"Teresa Tomeo's *Beyond Sunday* is an inspiring call to action for Catholics from all walks of life to fully embrace all the beauty and intelligence the Church has to offer."

— BISHOP ROBERT BARRON, author of *To Light a Fire on the Earth*

"The ultimate source of a full and abundant life — not a life of simply *existing* but a life in which the holes in our hearts are filled — is to let ourselves be loved by God. And this means seeking that life we were made to live. There is a supreme adventure awaiting us in this life. Teresa Tomeo's new book *Beyond Sunday* invites us to ignite this fire within and shows us, like a beacon, a practical way how. Everyone should read this book. Everyone."

— CHRIS STEFANICK, author, speaker,
and founder of Real Life Catholic

"With her clear passion for evangelization, Teresa Tomeo takes readers deeper into the Faith in such an engaging and accessible way. She equips us with the tools, not just to grow in our own relationship with God but to share our faith with friends and family. We're all meant to witness to Christ, and the more we let him into our lives, the more we can bring him into the world around us."

— EDWARD SRI, author of *Who Am I to Judge?*
and *Pope Francis and the Joy of the Gospel*

"Author Teresa Tomeo comes to the rescue by writing a book to encourage Catholics to live out their faith every day of the week, not reserving it for Sundays only. She points out that for many, faith is relegated to one hour a week on Sundays.... Tomeo wants to change this and guide folks to the true meaning of the Catholic Faith. *Beyond Sunday* is a breath of fresh air for today's Catholics and for all those who would like to learn more about the Catholic Church. In the author's own words, 'This book is designed to be a practical and honest look at where we've been and where we need to go.' I highly recommend this book and study guide!"

— DONNA-MARIE COOPER O'BOYLE, EWTN-TV host,
pilgrimage host, speaker, and award-winning and
best-selling author of more than twenty-five books,
including her memoir *The Kiss of Jesus:
How Mother Teresa and the Saints Helped
Me to Discover the Beauty of the Cross*

"In *Beyond Sunday*, Teresa Tomeo presents a refreshing solution to the age-old problem of Catholics who have members of their family that either have fallen away from their faith, don't go to Mass anymore, or are just going through the motions in order to fulfill their Sunday obligation. I applaud her for embracing Saint John Paul II's new evangelization by helping to reach the largest untapped market in the Church today. Through practical tips and humor, *Beyond Sunday* can appeal to all Catholics from different walks in life and help them grow in their relationship with Christ and open their eyes to the real beauty and treasures of the Catholic Faith."

— JANET MORANA, executive director, Priests for Life, and co-founder, Silent No More Awareness Campaign

"Teresa Tomeo has brought the Church something that is long overdue — a book that gives both cradle Catholics and converts the 'spiritual food' we all need to keep our faith alive and thriving! As a convert to the Faith, I was 'on fire' when I found THE CHURCH and came HOME. However, after twenty-five years, even though I am still a devout Catholic, I've noticed that the fire I once felt has become embers that are in need of stirring. Teresa's book is the poke that stirs that fire, and I am grateful that she has written it. Every Catholic, no matter where they are in their walk with our Lord, can benefit from this book."

— GAIL BUCKLEY, "The Bible Lady," founder and president of Catholic Scripture Study International

"From beginning to end, Teresa Tomeo offers insight on living our Catholic Faith every day of the week 'not to condemn but to encourage.' Wonderful practical ideas will help every reader find guides to holiness, step by step and day by day."

— FATHER MITCH PACWA, S.J., founder and president of Ignatius Productions, EWTN host, biblical scholar, author, and speaker

Beyond Sunday

Becoming a 24/7 Catholic

BEYOND Sunday

Becoming a
24/7 Catholic

TERESA TOMEO

Our Sunday Visitor

www.osv.com
Our Sunday Visitor Publishing Division
Our Sunday Visitor, Inc.
Huntington, Indiana 46750

ISBN: 978-1-68192-229-4 (Inventory No. T1931)
eISBN: 978-1-68192-230-0
LCCN: 2018934167

Cover and interior design: Lindsey Riesen
Cover art: Shutterstock

PRINTED IN THE UNITED STATES OF AMERICA

About the Author

TERESA TOMEO is a syndicated Catholic talk show host, an author of numerous books, and an international speaker. She has more than thirty years of experience in TV, radio, and newspapers, twenty of which were as a secular reporter/anchor in the Detroit market. Her weekday morning radio program, *Catholic Connection* — produced by Ave Maria Radio in Ann Arbor, Michigan, and the Eternal Word Television Network — can be heard on over five hundred radio stations worldwide and on the internet through the EWTN Global Catholic Radio Network. Teresa is a columnist and special correspondent for the national Catholic newspaper *OSV Newsweekly* and appears frequently on the EWTN Global Catholic Television Network. She co-hosts the EWTN television series *The Catholic View for Women* and is EWTN's field reporter for its annual March for Life coverage in Washington, D.C.

Teresa has been featured on *The O'Reilly Factor,* Fox News, *Fox & Friends,* MSNBC, *Dr. Laura*, and *Dr. James Dobson's Family Talk Radio*, discussing issues of faith, media awareness, and Catholic Church teaching, especially as it relates to the culture. She also hosts a monthly webinar, *Catholic Leaders Webinar Series: Media Matters*, produced by Our Sunday Visitor. Teresa owns her own speaking and communications company, Teresa Tomeo Communications, LLC. Teresa and her husband, Deacon Dominick Pastore, live in Michigan and speak around the world on the issue of marriage, based on their book, *Intimate Graces*. Connect with Teresa on her website/blog (www.TeresaTomeo.com), Facebook (@MrsTeresaTomeo), and Twitter (@TeresaTomeo).

Dedication

To my dear husband, Deacon Dominick Pastore, the one who showed me the way back to Jesus and the Church, enabling me to truly go beyond Sunday. And to my dear friend and fellow writer Gail Coniglio, the co-author of our *Beyond Sunday Study Guide*, whose input, guidance, and encouragement in this project made all the difference.

· ·

Special thanks also to Michele Chinault, from St. Mark the Evangelist Parish in Southwest Ranches, Florida, whose experience in Bible study and faith formation was invaluable in helping to make our Beyond Sunday program powerful and practical for all Catholics, no matter where they are in their journey.

Table of Contents

Foreword

Success in one of America's largest television markets had been suffocating Teresa Tomeo's once lively Catholic faith. She had grown inconsistent in Mass attendance, indifferent to virtue, and thoroughly uninterested in entering more deeply into the mysteries of the Faith. Ironically, under the hot camera lights, her faith had grown lukewarm, even cold. Sure, she still thought of herself as part of the Catholic tribe. Once a Catholic always a Catholic. It's like race or ethnicity, right? You may not go to Oktoberfest, but you are still German. Similarly, she still identified as a Catholic. But no jury would have convicted her of being one. Her Catholicism had become cultural, not personal.

Spiritual directors know this ailment as the common cold of Catholic minimalism and religious indifference. In Teresa's case, the cold was evolving into a fatal spiritual infection. She was close to drifting away from the Church altogether.

She wasn't alone. A vast number of American Catholics never develop a faith that flowers into more than obligatory Sunday Mass attendance. Many stop attending Mass altogether. Reasons abound: Mass is irrelevant and boring. Rather than feel hypocritical about inconsistent Mass attendance, it's easier not to go at all. Many would rather be shopping, golfing, visiting the grandkids, reading *The New York Times*, watching the Sunday news programs. Mass is hard to understand. Many don't fully believe the Creed we recite each week. Many do not feel fully a part of their parish family, and maybe they don't really want to feel that way. Over the last generation, more and more Catholics have drifted away, until "former" or "ex"-Catholics constitute the second-largest religious body in America.

When Teresa's marriage came under threat, she finally recognized the spiritual dimension of her problem. She wasn't interested in scolding priests, bishops, her husband, relatives, or friends. She took responsibility for her spiritual life. In her job, she had grown into a mature, respected journalist carefully practicing the tools of her trade. But in the most important area of her life, her soul, she had remained a baby Christian whose head was filled with childish beliefs and whose conscience remained unformed and flabby. She knew she needed more.

Her personal renewal and revival led to a reformation and rebuilding of her life. She is passionate to share the insights that transformed her life and marriage, and turned her career into a ministry. When she finally decided to reconsider what Christ teaches through his Body, the Church, she discovered the great adventure of going beyond Sunday as a Catholic. She found that she had been called and gifted for service. God promised that if she went deeper, her service would grow wider.

First, she focused on forming a disciple's heart. Revival began within herself. Reform continued in her home and marriage. But God wasn't stopping there. Teresa discovered the joys of Catholic service in her own backyard, in her local church community. And, in time, through her apostolic labors, in tandem with her now deacon husband, Dominick, she ministered to the worldwide Catholic communion. Christ was faithful, even when she had been faithless. He not only healed her marriage but formed a servant's heart within her.

We may not all be called to worldwide ministry. But we are all called to live a distinct Catholic way of life, a life that reflects the priorities of the kingdom of God. Teresa knows you can only find that way of life by going beyond Sunday. In this book and program, you'll be challenged to get real and take a spiritual inventory of your current wants and needs.

What can you legitimately expect God to do in your life? You'll learn that spiritual disciplines are not burdensome. Did you know that something as simple as reading a short chapter of Scripture a day will immediately begin to enrich your life? Would you like to converse with God? Would you like to actually pray and not just "say prayers"? Not just talk, but listen? *Beyond Sunday* will show you how. Teresa's breezy and candid style highlights a host of practical points designed to transform you into a 24/7 Catholic, a disciple, a learner in the school of Jesus Christ. He designed you to flourish for eternity. So why not start today by going *beyond Sunday*?

— AL KRESTA
CEO of Ave Maria Radio,
host of *Kresta in the Afternoon*,
apologist, author, and speaker

INTRODUCTION

Living a Truly Abundant Life

....

"I came that they may have life, and have it abundantly."
— JOHN 10:10

A few years ago, as part of a professional growth seminar, my husband and other executives at his architectural engineering firm were asked to read Jim Collins' book *Good to Great: Why Some Companies Make the Leap and Others Don't.* The book, which was based on extensive research of top companies that made the leap from good to great and sustained that greatness over the long term, had a very positive effect on my husband, and not only on a professional level. There were so many parallels between a company making the efforts and changes to be the best in its field and a Christian trying to live the Gospel faithfully. Take, for example, this quote: "Few people attain great lives, in large part because it is just so easy to settle for a good life."

If you're reading this book, chances are you have come to realize that a "good" life is simply not enough. As Christians, we're called to something even better. The Gospel of John tells us what God wants for each and every one of us: not just a "so-so," mediocre, or even a good life, but a great life, complete with long-lasting joy. This is what will not only satisfy our deepest personal longings but will in turn allow us to make a difference and leave a legacy.

That's why going beyond Sunday is so important, because deep down, isn't that what we all want? Even if our faith life is pretty good, why settle for that when we could have a faith life that is great? And this abundance is available to us, if we have the courage to tap into it. When we are truly happy, when the deepest longings of our heart are being addressed, when those big questions that keep cropping up about why we're here and where we're going are answered, our direction is clear. We experience true purpose and meaning. True joy and happiness are contagious in a good way. They bubble over into all areas of our lives and send positive ripple effects into our own circles and beyond.

And that's why I wrote this book. *Beyond Sunday* is about obtaining true *greatness*, not in terms of business or worldly success, but from God's perspective. This is everything. And as I have learned from many years of studying at the school of hard knocks, it's the only thing.

In 2004, during his World Youth Day address to young people, Pope John Paul II, now a Catholic saint, urged the youth to begin the greatest quest of their lives, imitating a group of Greek people mentioned in the Gospel of John: "So these came to Philip, who was from Bethsaida in Galilee, and said to him, 'Sir, we wish to see Jesus' " (Jn 12:21). The pope said:

> I want you too to imitate those "Greeks" who spoke to Philip, moved by a desire to "see Jesus." May your search be motivated not simply by intellectual curiosity, though that too is something positive, but be stimulated above all by an inner urge to find the answer to the question about the meaning of your life.... The desire to see Jesus dwells deep in the heart of each man and each woman. My dear young people, allow Jesus to gaze into your eyes so that the desire to see the Light, and to experience the splendor of the Truth, may grow within you.[1]

This book is my personal invitation to you to "see Jesus" and the Catholic Church like never before. It is my hope that, reading this book, you will encounter God in a whole new way, not just in the pew on Sunday, but every day of the week. I am so excited about the effort of going beyond Sunday, and all that it has to offer you, that I want to shout from the housetops: "Come on in! The water is not just fine — it's fantastic!"

Okay, so my enthusiasm might seem a little corny or maybe a little out there, but I just can't help it. I am so very grateful that someone who made so many mistakes (yes, that would be me) has been given so many second, third, and fourth chances, and I want to show that gratitude by again extending an invitation. It is okay if you don't feel ready to dive into the pool head first. I get it, and I have been there. Hopefully, though, what you find on the following pages will encourage you to do more than just stick your spiritual toes in the water. It's my sincere prayer that eventually you will want to immerse yourself as I did, let go of the ladder, and swim. Or, as that old cliché puts it, "Let go and let God."

We don't ever have to be afraid of sinking or drowning. That's because, wherever we're at in the journey, God loves us — you, me, every one of us, right where we are. He's the number one lifeguard in the universe.

....

"I would rather have thirty minutes of wonderful than a lifetime of nothing special." — *Steel Magnolias*

....

Many years ago, my faith journey left me a bit empty, and I was lost. The world told me that it was all about me, and in particular, as a woman growing up in the 1960s and '70s and entering the very competitive and extremely demanding career of broadcast news in the early '80s, that it was all about the career. Nothing else mattered — not family, and certainly not faith. Full speed ahead. Whatever it takes to be successful.

I was raised Catholic and still believed in God, but I really didn't understand (or, quite frankly, didn't feel a need to understand) more about him than going to weekly Mass, if that. As the title of this book suggests, I never took my faith "beyond Sunday." Through lots of ups, downs, twists, turns, and personal challenges that I will share later, this lost sheep finally made her way back.

Eventually, I came to realize I was needing more direction in my life and wanted to go deeper into my faith. Something told me I was missing out, despite my worldly success, and I was looking for more. I wondered how one goes about practically applying faith to everyday activities and decisions while still living a balanced life. What does that really look like? Does it mean walking around in sackcloth and ashes or never meeting friends for happy hour again because you're spending all of your spare time at the local parish? If any of these scenarios were true, I would be in big trouble. I really enjoy clothes, as well as a good glass of wine and the occasional happy hour. Thankfully, I learned that living my faith with more intention does not necessarily mean giving these things up. In fact, I can honestly say I am having more fun in my life now than I ever did in my days as a nominal Catholic, and I don't want to keep this all to myself. It's too amazing. God and his Church have so much to offer.

Early in his pontificate, Pope Francis reminded Catholics that we need not be pickled-pepper Christians. After all, who wants to hang around with a bunch of sour-faced folks? A godly life is one of joy and, yes, that includes plenty of good, clean fun — not to mention, some good vino. Oh, and by the way, I never met a mall I didn't like. Or a sale that didn't have my name on it.

I'm really glad you've picked up this book. And I hope that once you are done reading it, you'll pass this information on to others. I am excited that you are joining me on this journey of going beyond Sunday.

A Road Traveled by One Too Many

In his famous poem "The Road Not Taken," Robert Frost happily tells us that he took the road less traveled. If only that were the case for so many of us who were raised in the Church. While everyone's particular circumstances are different, over the years I've run into so many Catholics who have struggles very much like those I experienced, and I suspect like yours as well. I was baptized into the Faith as an infant and grew up going to Mass with my family. I even attended Catholic school. Yet I didn't see my faith having much to do with my life after Mass each weekend. At one point in my life, I was one of those Catholics who had fallen away from my faith completely. So, as one who has walked this journey herself, I hope that sharing my story will provide encouragement and hope as you step out in faith.

It's been said by some Catholic converts that "cradle Catholics" are sitting on a spiritual Fort Knox, and they don't even know it. This is partly because, for generations, most of the culture shared the same moral values as the Catholic Church, and there was a certain comfort level that came along with that. As Archbishop Allen H. Vigneron of my Archdiocese of Detroit details in his 2017 pastoral letter, *Unleash the Gospel*, there is not as much urgency in a message when it's understood that most appreciate and agree with that message. As a result, sadly, "parishes and dioceses slipped almost imperceptibly into a mode of maintenance rather than mission. Many Catholics came to think of evangelization as a special calling, primarily for priests and religious in the foreign missions."[2]

The shifts in the culture over the past sixty years have made it clear that we need to revisit our understanding of the Church, of its place in the world, and of our role as Catholic Christians. In other words, many of us in the Church today need what Saint John Paul II referred to as "the new evangelization." The mission fields aren't just faraway places where people with a special call to be missionaries can go take care of the poor and spread the Faith. We ourselves need to be evangelized. We need to hear the Good News, especially those of us who have grown up in the Church but have never really gotten past going through the motions.

We live in a high-tech information age, and it might be a bit of an exaggeration, but just about anything and everything you ever wanted to know about the Catholic Church (and Christianity in general) can be found at the click of a mouse. The entire *Catechism of the Catholic Church* is free and readily accessible online, not to mention countless Catholic ministries, apostolates, Bible studies, papal documents, podcasts, radio shows, books, and personal testimonies. The list of available resources is (and this is not a stretch by any means) pretty much endless. Yet too many of us have no idea these resources even exist. Many are drowned out or overshadowed by everything else that's out there, from the twenty-four-hour news cycle to social media, pop culture outlets, and anything else that's got a hold of our time and attention. (By the way, you'll find some of my favorite Catholic resources in a detailed list in the appendix of this book.)

Let's take a quick stroll down memory (or history) lane to get a better understanding of just how much cultural norms have changed today from twenty, thirty, or fifty years ago. The so-called sexual revolution that began in the 1960s occurred at the same time that the mass media exploded onto the world stage. This was an explosion of very loud and consistent voices that were, and still are, busy painting Christianity — and especially Catholic Christianity — as backward and oppressive, while touting the values and norms of the sexual revolution as the only true way to freedom and happiness. The sudden prevalence of the "me" culture coupled with the mass media gave the microphones and megaphones to people with a very different message, often directly opposed to the teachings of the Church. And far too often, the Church's voice got drowned out in an increasingly fast-paced and noisy culture, driven by the media. Meanwhile, the culture itself shifted to one of instant gratification and "it's whatever I want and feel," which naturally became more and more hostile to basic Catholic principles. The idea of embracing suffering and picking up your cross daily became a foreign one to many. Living out the virtues as a wholesome Catholic in today's society has continued to become more and more unpopular. This has caused many to hold back from living out their faith with courage.

Fast forward to today, and we see the fallout. Only about 24 percent of the more than seventy million Americans who still identify as Catholic attend weekly Mass. And for many Mass-going Catholics, that hour each week is basically the only time during the week when they're hearing about God. Compare that to what they're hearing on a daily basis from mass media, social media, advertisements, and the culture at large. No wonder it's difficult for so many of us Catholics today to go beyond Sunday.

Stop and think for a moment about the relationships in your life. You probably have at least a few relatives and friends whom you love deeply and with whom you're very close. These are committed relationships. You've invested, and continue to invest, a great deal of time, sacrifice, and effort because of the love you have for them. These relationships were built over time as you got to know them more intimately.

Now think of the casual acquaintances in your life. You know "of" them through association. You may see them or come in contact with them even somewhat regularly in your comings and goings. But because you are somewhat removed from them, the relationship isn't very deep or very strong. Maybe it has reduced to just a Christmas card exchange every year.

Finally, think about your relationship with God. He wants us to be his intimate friends, but for many of us God is more like a casual acquaintance. God is our creator and knows us better than anyone else. The concept of bringing God and our faith into our everyday life has rarely been truly explained or, more importantly, made evident by the actions of the people around us. We see God off on the sidelines somewhere and not as a major player in the game called life. And most of us don't really know what to do to fix that.

That's where I was many years ago. Looking back, I realize that even though I did not have bad intentions, I found myself relegating faith to one hour per week. I hadn't left the Church by any means. My husband and I wanted to practice our faith, but we just didn't really feel like we had the knowledge or the ability to live our faith beyond doing what we know we're "supposed to": going to church on Sunday.

For far too many Catholics, faith is mostly defined by Mass attendance. Many Catholics have no real, flesh-and-blood examples of what "beyond Sunday" means or looks like. For the older generation, faith means weekly Mass; for the millennials, baby boomers, and others, faith means Mass attendance on major holidays, if at all.

This book is designed to be a practical and honest look at where we've been and where we need to go. I've heard from folks around the country — whether at speaking events or among radio followers — that they felt judged or unwelcomed by the Catholics who are very involved at the parish level. They don't feel "holy" enough or educated enough in the Faith to participate in other activities outside of Mass. They feel like they're back in high school, being rejected by the "in" crowd. Let me just say, I'm very sorry if you've been made to feel that way in any church setting, whether that's your local parish or a church you have visited in the past. Please know, you have every right to be involved, and it doesn't matter how much you know about your faith. We're all always learning more. Your journey is just as important as anyone else's. Don't let your sense of being unwanted or unworthy keep you from God — the truth is, he does want you. Very, very much.

Hopefully this book will help you start digging a little deeper, no matter where you are in your journey today.

It may surprise you to hear that even if you go to Mass every week and hear the Bible readings, you still might not know the Gospel of Jesus. Being somewhat familiar with someone and having a deep, committed relationship with him or her are two very different things. That was the case with me and my husband growing up Catholic, and it's not an exaggeration to say it's the case with a large majority of Catholics, including those who are in the pews regularly. God is the only one who can judge hearts. And God, who created us, understands us better than we understand ourselves. Therefore, he realizes we can't love him without truly "knowing" him.

Getting to know Jesus and our faith on a personal level actually makes a lot of difference when it comes to true happiness. Yes, God loves us right where we're at. But as I heard a preacher say once, he also loves us enough not to keep us there. Why settle for a so-so relationship with God, when you can have a great relationship with him that is filled with abundant joy? That's right, abundant joy, as Jesus reminds us: "I came that they may have life, and have it abundantly" (Jn 10:10).

Don't all of us deserve a chance at an abundant life? That's what God wants for all of us. It is what he has prepared for each of us by giving us the gift of the Church. He has so much more in store for us. He wants to fulfill the longing rather than leave us scratching our heads, feeling like we're missing out on something truly wonderful. This is no small task. It takes time, patience, and effort. But it's so worth it.

As a matter of fact, there is nothing in your life that could ever top an active, living, breathing relationship with the one who created us and knows us better than we know ourselves. Hey, I'm a Catholic talk show host. Would I lie to you? And not just any talk show host: I am a talk show host married to a man who is now a Catholic deacon, believe it or not. I'm a Catholic talk show host who, in her previous life, had everything according to the world's standards and was still miserable. Both my husband and I are living proof that the journey of faith is so worth it.

This journey could lead you to reinvent yourself, not only spiritually and personally, but even possibly professionally as well. That's what happened to us. Don't let that frighten you! God may or may not have something like that in mind for you, and he knows exactly what's best for you. Just remember that God is not going to abandon you. He has a plan — a plan that is so much better than the one we've invented for ourselves. Trust me when I say: Been there, done that, and bought the T-shirt. And while my husband and I absolutely love this re-invention or extreme makeover God did in our lives, we're most grateful for what he did in our marriage, giving new life to a relationship in near ruins. That's reason enough to write not only this book but countless others.

This is a book about encouragement and not condemnation. Considering I spent many a year as a dazed and confused nominal Catholic Christian, I am certainly in no position to point fingers. And while this book will take a look back to see what might have gone wrong in the evangelization and catechesis categories, it doesn't stay stuck in the past, whining about what might have been. Instead, I am hoping this book in some small way will serve as motivation or inspiration to help you take the next step in your own walk of faith.

This book is for Catholic Christians who want to discover the fullness of the Faith and truly make it a part of their daily lives. More than that, it's for Catholics who want to ensure their lives have deep meaning and who want to help make the world a better place in some way. It's for Catholics who want to help pass on a living faith to those coming up behind us. And last but not least, it's for Catholics who are already happily hanging out in the faith pool but realize that there is more to life than floating or coasting along.

CHAPTER ONE

Outside the Box

Taking Faith Beyond Our Comfort Zone

....

*"You have to change your thinking if you desire to
have a future different from your present."*
— GERMANY KENT

For many years, I kept God and my faith in a neat little box. The box was very attractive because it was convenient and comfortable. It was comforting to know it was there if I needed it — basically, only in emergencies. I closed my faith box during the week and opened it only on Sundays, when I went to Mass and closed it again after I came home from Mass. Within a few short months after I entered college, I had even stopped going to weekly Mass. There were those emergency moments when I would rush back to the local parish on campus with the lovely little faith box in hand. When my prayers were answered, though, the box went back into hiding. All was right with the world, or so I thought.

This attitude toward God and my Catholic faith didn't happen overnight. There wasn't one incident that catapulted me out of the Church. I was simply too involved in trying to forge a path for myself in the very competitive field of news broadcasting. Competing for coveted news internships, working at the radio station, and writing for the campus newspaper took up all of my time. Soon God just didn't fit into my life anymore. It was a gradual drifting and desensitization. I still identified myself as Catholic if classmates or friends asked about my religious affiliation. But God just wasn't at the top of my priority list.

My parents had spent a nice chunk of change sending me and my sisters to Catholic school. Thank the good Lord it was an excellent school that taught the Faith well. You might be wondering, "Well, if they did such a good job, why did you fall away from your faith?" For me, personally, the pull of the world was too strong. My teachers, both lay and religious, were very good at encouraging vocations, and not only vocations to the priesthood or religious life. They spotted my gift for gab when I was only in the third grade, and they decided to do their best to help me learn how to use that gift wisely. That led to small parts in school plays, forensics, and debate competitions. When I stepped inside my local high school, I walked almost immediately into the guidance counselor's office to tell her that I had already chosen communications, and in particular broadcast journalism, as my field of interest. From there, I started working on the high school radio station and newspaper. Things were going just as I had planned and hoped.

Since I was still living at home, regular Mass attendance was a must. I obliged my parents but really didn't give the God thing much thought beyond that, as everything was going so nicely and according to plan. At that point in my life, my faith box was still sitting on the dresser or table, so to speak, where I could grab it quickly if needed, but it remained for the most part closed.

Slowly, the box was placed up on a shelf inside a closet — out of sight, out of mind. Really, I was only open to the limited ideas I had of what faith looked like for an independent career girl like me. For decades that box was kept in the tiniest corner of my heart. Kind of like that old box of trinkets or mementos that are too special to throw out but also not very useful or appropriate in one's current life. We hide it away, only to be recovered when we need an emotional boost or a warm and fuzzy nostalgic moment.

And inside my faith box, I did find some warm and fuzzy spiritual things, such as memories of growing up and attending Catholic grade school. I get teary eyed thinking about my experience of receiving Holy Communion for the very first time. The nuns had given us strict instructions on how to process down the long aisle of our church, how to sit, and how to receive Communion. What if I did something wrong?

And then there was that darned veil. Both my dress and veil were hand-me-downs from my older sister, who didn't happen to have as much hair as yours truly. I could not for the life of me get my veil to stay put on my head. I was a nervous wreck. But I turned around and looked up at the choir loft and saw my dad smiling down at me with a look of pride on his handsome face. And then I looked back toward the altar and saw the beautiful image of Jesus, with his arms outstretched in a welcoming gesture.

I definitely had some warm and fuzzy God moments that over the years I could pull out of the box because I knew they would bring a smile to my face. And getting back to those wonderful teachers I had, there were also the fond memories of the sisters and lay teachers at my Catholic grade school. They showed a lot of patience and love toward a young girl who frequently got into trouble for talking too much in class.

A little deeper in my faith box were the foxhole prayers: the prayers I pulled out when I was frustrated or anxious. I would often say them in college on the night before a big exam or when sitting in my dorm room, just waiting for that cute guy in my political science class to finally give me a call: "Oh, please, God. I promise I will get back to Mass and be a good Catholic if you just answer this one prayer for me."

Later in my life, the foxhole prayers pertained to career goals, taking the professional wish list out of the box, insisting that God bless that list and affirm it exactly as I saw fit. My box also contained the occasional formula prayer, such as the Hail Mary or the Lord's Prayer. Mass was in there, too, but it was mostly reserved for Christmas and Easter, or when my parents came to visit.

Inevitably, after I had my brief God moment, everything would go back in the box, and the box would get buried once again, hidden behind all the other stuff I considered so much more important. The pattern of keeping God and my faith neatly and tightly packed away in a box had become routine. I was far too sophisticated and modern to need God for more than the occasional pick-me-up or 911 call.

This inside-the-box faith approach lasted until my early thirties, several years into my marriage and a high-profile media career. Sounds cliché but, basically, I hit rock bottom. It's as if one day I woke up, finally started to look around, and everything I had spent so much time and effort building was crumbling. I had sacrificed so much of my personal life for my profession, giving up holidays, weekends, and nights at home. I ran into work for what seemed like every breaking news story, telling myself that because I had a supportive and loving husband, everything at home would be fine. After all, he was also very career-oriented, moving up the ladder quickly at his engineering firm. He worked a lot of extra hours, especially on weekends. We both had swallowed the yuppie (young urban professional) way of life. This is what was drilled into us back then, especially career-minded women. I have to say, looking back, that I was the more aggressive one. My husband started to feel that we were like the proverbial gerbils on the wheel, constantly running and getting nowhere fast.

You might be wondering what caused me to hit rock bottom and to wake up and finally realize that my life was literally going to hell in a handbasket. Well, some of us are more stubborn than others, and in order for God to get my attention, he had to take me out of my comfort zone, big time.

My first major "come to Jesus" moment happened when I was stripped of what I unfortunately held most dear: my job. To make a long story short, one day I was the lead story on the evening news. The next morning, I received a phone call from the assignment editor asking me to come in early. Given the size of my ego at the time, I just assumed the station had another major assignment that only I could handle, so I eagerly hopped out of bed and headed into the office early. To my surprise, within less than an hour, I was walking out of the station with a pink slip and a box of my personal belongings in my hands.

That was all I had to show for all of those very long days, nights, and weekends; all I had to show for the many sacrifices I had made in my personal life. The news director and station manager were making changes in the on-air team, and I was one of them. My contract was up for renewal, but since I hadn't heard any bad news from my agent, I expected that it was only a matter of time before I was once again signing on the dotted line. Just the opposite happened. I ended up on the cutting room floor, along with several other staff members.

Given the volatile nature of the news business, I shouldn't have been so shocked. The broadcasting business is brutal, and there's an old line among broadcasters that TV and radio stations are pretty much equipped with revolving doors because changing and replacing on-air talent is practically an everyday occurrence. But when you build your entire world around your career, and that career takes a huge hit, it feels as if your world is crumbling.

At the time I thought my world could never be put back together. I thought it was the worst thing that could ever happen to me. But it ended up being a major blessing in disguise. It was the start of my long path back to healing both my marriage and my relationship with God. My husband and I had grown far apart, and my relationship with God was practically nonexistent. As painful as the firing experience was, the time off of work was crucial when it came to stepping outside my comfort zone and taking a good, long look at myself and my priorities — or lack thereof.

Here's a news flash, something that it took me way too long to learn: God doesn't belong in a box. What's more, there isn't a box on the planet immense enough for who he is and how much he loves us. Saint Paul reminds us of this: "O the depth of the riches and wisdom and knowledge of God! How unsearchable are his judgments and how inscrutable his ways!" (Rom 11:33). The prophet Isaiah also tells us "good luck" in trying to put omnipotence in a nice little package:

Have you not known? Have you not heard?
The LORD is the everlasting God,
   the Creator of the ends of the earth.
He does not faint or grow weary,
   his understanding is unsearchable. (Is 40:28)

Sadly, leaving our faith in a comfortable container, never allowing it to be part of our lives beyond Sunday (if we even take it as far Sunday Mass) has become the norm rather than the exception.

So now would be a good time to start examining your own faith box, to take a closer look at its size, its contents, and its location. Where do you keep that box? In many ways, it is understandable why that box might be kept under the bed, on a shelf, or in the shed. We let so many other things take priority.

Think about the important relationships in your life, as well as the most important activities. These are people, issues, or efforts to which you're dedicated. They are not tucked in a box that is packed away somewhere. You grow to love someone by spending time with them. You're passionate about your work or a particular cause because you have learned a great deal about these things and why they make a difference. Think about what your faith life, and in particular your relationship with God, might be like if you took a similar approach. If you're already going to Mass once a week, have you ever thought about getting to church a little earlier to have some quiet time with God? Can you give him just a little bit more of your time and attention?

Maybe you were raised to believe that faith is a private or personal matter. Catholics, especially, did not, and still often do not, see themselves as evangelists, even though ironically that's the reason the Catholic Church exists. Yes, the Church exists to evangelize, as Pope Saint Paul VI (who will be canonized in 2018) reminded the world in his apostolic exhortation *Evangelization in the Modern World*:

> "We wish to confirm once more that the task of evangelizing all people constitutes the essential mission of the Church" (*"Declaration of the Synod Fathers,"* 4: *L'Osservatore Romano* [October 27, 1974], p. 6). It is a task and mission which the vast and profound changes of present-day society make all the more urgent. Evangelizing is in fact the grace and vocation proper to the Church, her deepest identity. She exists in order to evangelize.[3]

Yet when a lot of us were growing up, much of the world agreed with the basic tenets of Christianity, so we really didn't see a need to open the box or build a bigger and better one.

If this describes you, here's where you can begin to move a bit outside that comfort zone. The first step is to think a little harder and a little differently. Seeing or treating faith as a private or personal thing is kind of a strange approach, isn't it, if we know anything at all about the Gospel? The word "gospel" means "good news," and good news is meant to be shared. When was the last time you kept a piece of really good news to yourself? So, actually, it's odd that many of us were raised to keep the best news and the greatest story ever told to ourselves.

That said, evangelization comes later. Yes, we all have that responsibility, but when and how we evangelize takes some time, prayer, and discernment. It's not all that different from other efforts in our lives. How many new parents do you know who right away go around sharing their parenting tips? Most new moms and dads are doing just the opposite: asking for help, advice, and input from more experienced parents. They learn, and eventually they share.

The primary way to share our faith is to live it to the best of our ability and with real joy. That's what this book is all about. And as you begin to take further steps outside of your comfort zone, I encourage you to start thinking differently about what evangelization means and looks like.

There are plenty of ways to proclaim the Good News. Not everyone is called to stand on a soapbox in Central Park or at the local town hall, or even share on Facebook or Twitter. (Though, for the record, Pope Francis has one of the largest Twitter followings on the planet. Just saying.) Yes, we're all called to evangelize, but evangelization comes in all shapes and sizes. You just need to find yours. It most likely will mean some movement and change in your life, but don't panic. Remember, everyone is on a different journey, and we get there when we get there. We just have to be willing to take the faith box out of hiding and move, maybe slowly at first, but eventually, to a better place.

What's in Your Faith Box? Taking Inventory

There is an old saying: "Good things come in small packages. And so does poison." I think this is key to understanding what can happen in our lives — and, most importantly, in our hearts and minds — when we attempt to put God in a box and keep him at a safe distance. When we keep him at arm's length, or even farther, we make ourselves extremely vulnerable to influences, messages, and ideologies that can — again speaking from personal experience — "poison" us.

If I was heavily influenced by the culture back in the 1970s, '80s, and '90s — before we had Facebook, Twitter, Instagram, hundreds of satellite channels, iPhones, iPads, iWatches, etc. — then how much more are we being formed by media today? It's not that we are bad people, or that the people behind the messages we're getting bombarded with constantly are bad, either (only God can judge hearts, after all). Yet the messages we receive from all sides are not designed to give us true joy and inner peace. They tell us that materialism, sex without attachment, and professional success (just to name a few) equal total fulfillment and happiness. But anyone who has gone down that road, including me, will tell you these things alone don't bring happiness. Instant gratification is gone as fast as we attain it. And once it's gone, we're running on empty.

I was running on empty and going nowhere fast. It wasn't until my life was spinning out of control that I finally cried out for help, and things slowly began to change. The soul-searching, along with the job search, lasted for some six months. At that point, my husband and I realized things had to change. If we were going to save our marriage, we needed help. Most importantly — and I believe this was our Catholic roots coming to the surface — we realized that we needed God in our lives. We made a commitment to get some counseling.

As I mentioned, my husband had already felt that we needed to address our fast-paced, and what proved to be empty, lifestyle. Since I was too busy at first to notice his discontentment, I went on my merry way, continuing at a very hectic pace. In the meantime, he was invited to a men's Bible study by a mutual friend. It was a study that had a huge impact on his life and was actually the initial catalyst of our return to the Church. In the pages of Scripture, he rediscovered the Catholic Church and began to take classes at Sacred Heart Major Seminary in the Archdiocese of Detroit. Years later, this would eventually lead him to discern becoming a deacon. But that was a long way off.

In the meantime, after I lost my job, even though I agreed that we needed counseling and also agreed that we should start to take our faith seriously, deep down I was angry with God. Seems kind of silly, don't you think? I really had no relationship with God, but I was angry with him and secretly blamed him for my problems. The really big turning point came when I simply cried uncle. I was finally getting a clue that God is God and I am not. My prayer certainly wasn't sophisticated. I just prayed really hard, out of desperation.

God answered those prayers in a number of different ways, one of which was a job offer at another local TV station, which I eventually took. That's when the real work began, though, because as my priorities changed and faith became the central part of my life, my career also changed. Joining the Bible study with my husband, getting back to Mass every week, and learning how to pray resulted in the scales falling from my eyes and me feeling very differently about the news business.

If you're reading this book, you're probably aware of these feelings in your own heart, and you are looking for answers. You're looking for something substantial to satisfy the longings, something that won't leave you empty. You might not be in as rough shape as I was emotionally and spiritually when I finally let God into my life, but why wait for that?

As this chapter closes, let me leave you with some thoughts from TV and film star Jim Caviezel. Caviezel, you may recall, played the starring role in the blockbuster film *The Passion of the Christ*.

In January 2018, he gave a powerful address to a group of Catholic college students and young adults gathered in Chicago for the annual FOCUS (the Fellowship of Catholic University Students) conference. The theme of the address was to encourage us not to be afraid to grow in our faith. Growth in faith not only frees us to live a better and more fulfilled life ourselves but also allows us to make a difference.

Caviezel spoke personally about the extreme responsibilities and challenges, both emotional and physical, of portraying Christ. While filming the Crucifixion scenes, he actually suffered, among many other things, a dislocated shoulder and getting struck by lightning.

The film was shot in an ancient mountain town of southern Italy, the historic town of Matera. My husband and I have been to this town twice. In 2017, we actually took a tour based on the filming of *The Passion*. The rugged hilltop where the Crucifixion scene was shot and the cobblestone path leading up to that very stark location are both part of that tour. Standing there, looking out over the hillside, gives you the sense of how difficult it must have been for the film crew, given the ruggedness of the land. Just walking up, down, and around the area on a nice fall day, as we were, was difficult at times.

But in the end, Caviezel says, his performance would not have been nearly as convincing if he hadn't been literally stretched beyond his comfort zone: "But had this been shot in a studio, you never would have seen that performance. The suffering made the performance, just as it makes our lives."

Life will never go according to your plans, hopes, and dreams if you stay in your comfort zone. We get that when it comes to working hard to land that new job, making sacrifice after sacrifice to save for college tuition or a new home, or taking that first crack at parenting. Think not only about the efforts you made during those extremely challenging times, along with the risks you took, but also about the positive results.

Of course, no one's life is perfect. We all have our ups and downs. You were probably pretty darn scared at those crucial points in your life. You probably had more than one of your own "Caviezel" moments on a different type of cross. But looking back, aren't you glad that you decided to push through the tough times and go for it? Despite the occasional disappointments and struggles, there is no doubt that moving out of the comfort zone is the only way to really live.

The same guts and gusto need to be applied to the next step in your faith life. The search will definitely take you out of your comfort zone. But remember, Jesus came to comfort the afflicted and afflict the comfortable. And as in all of those other important areas of our lives, as Jim Caviezel told those college students, that "affliction" makes all the difference.

MONDAY

Pray & Reflect: Come, Holy Spirit! (What led you to this book? Where is your faith box right now, and how open is it?)

TUESDAY

Pray: When you wake up, offer the day to God and ask him to help you see more clearly his will for your life.

WEDNESDAY

Act: What one thing can you do this week to move out of your faith comfort zone?

THURSDAY

Act: Take a step out in faith and act upon the one thing God is asking you to do to get out of your comfort zone.

FRIDAY

Reflect: Think about the steps you took this week to move out of your comfort zone. What did you learn about yourself and about God?

SATURDAY

Read & Reflect: Read and reflect on the readings for this Sunday, which you can find at www.usccb.org/bible/readings.

CHAPTER TWO

The Church as Field Hospital

....

Jesus went about all the cities and villages,
teaching in their synagogues and preaching the gospel of the kingdom,
and healing every disease and every infirmity.
— MATTHEW 9:35

Pope Francis reminds us regularly that the Church is not a sanctuary for saints but a hospital of sorts for those in need. Whew. I don't know about you, but that sure makes me feel better. Okay, so nobody's perfect. As a deacon friend of mine always says, "Everybody's got something." Or as I like to say, if we're still here, then God is not through with us yet. So, we're all in this together, here to help each be the best we can be.

If we want to get in better shape, whether it's with our finances, our waistline, our car that needs fine-tuning, or our house that might be a fixer-upper, we have to identify what needs the shaping, fine-tuning, and fixing. What could we be doing differently or more efficiently that will have a positive effect? In other words, we have to diagnose the issue.

I am not too proud to say that I have had a lot of issues in terms of my walk with God. This is why I know it's so important to talk about what I refer to as *common Catholic ailments*. These are issues or stumbling blocks to the Faith that we encounter as we grow in faith. I can't go into every type of ailment here, but I will focus on some that I and others close to me have experienced in some way. Identifying these ailments in myself has helped me to address them.

At one time or another in my life, I have had all of the common Catholic ailments I'm about to address here. As a matter of fact, these ailments almost did me in. They sent me to the spiritual emergency room more than once, so you'd think I'd have gotten the hint after a while. Some of us are just a bit slower than others. Deep down I think I knew where I could find the ultimate cure, but I was too stubborn and prideful, and too determined to get better on my own or to "do it my way," as Frank Sinatra ("Ol' Blue Eyes") used to sing.

Let's think about this from a physical health perspective. When we want to protect ourselves from, say, getting a nasty bout of the flu or a bad cold, what do we do? We try to take good care of ourselves by getting enough sleep, washing our hands regularly, taking vitamins, and staying away from things that might weaken our immune system. We don't walk outside in the dead of winter without wearing a hat, for example. And we get the flu shot once a year. The medical community also continues to study the impact illnesses have on our physical well-being in order to create more effective remedies.

It's the same way with our spiritual ailments. The more we know how and why they happen, the better equipped we are to prevent them from occurring again and again.

An examination or overview of these ailments is not meant to criticize, mock, or condemn anyone. Instead, I hope it will serve both as a needed diagnosis for many and as preventative medicine. Besides, there's this important truth to keep in mind: as the pope tells us, the Church is not a sanctuary for saints but a hospital for sinners.

To be quite blunt, this review of common Catholic ailments is a good, long look in the mirror for me. I am very familiar with each of these ailments. Actually, I feel like I invented all of them. And if you're a cradle Catholic, born and raised in the Faith like me, you've probably been hit with at least a mild case of one of them at one time or another, or know someone who has. Here they are:

- Holy Osmosis
- Christeritis
- Only-on-Sunday Syndrome
- Chronic Catholic Curmudgeonitis

Holy Osmosis

I first heard about this ailment during a radio interview I was doing with Catholic apologist Karl Keating. Karl founded Catholic Answers, a Catholic apologetics ministry that includes a daily live call-in show on Catholic radio, along with books, conferences, and online efforts dedicated to educating people in the Catholic Faith. A listener phoning in to my program that day raised the same question that a lot of us have raised many times — one of the big questions I am hoping to answer in this book: Why don't Catholics know more about the Faith?

You may have asked that question yourself several times, or scratched your head over the fact that someone could spend eight or even twelve years in Catholic school, yet, if pressed, would barely be able to name the four Gospel writers or the seven sacraments.

According to the Oxford Dictionary, *osmosis* is "the process of gradual or unconscious assimilation of ideas and knowledge." Holy osmosis, as Karl explained it on the radio, refers to the prevalent attitude in the Church that somehow all of us would soak up the Faith by going through the motions. There was a certain formula or system set in place before the Second Vatican Council (a time when society still reflected and supported Christian morality). Moms and dads did their best to make sure their children got a Catholic education. The family went to Mass together on Sunday. If parents couldn't afford private school, the children would be dropped off at catechism class once a week. And since, for the most part, parents didn't have as much moral bankruptcy to deal with, it didn't seem like much more needed to be done. Somehow, through some kind of Catholic education, the Faith would be soaked up and practiced.

However, that faith formula was not able to withstand the forces of culture that came crashing into the world and our parishes, beginning with the so-called sexual revolution in the 1960s.

And this is why the point of going "beyond Sunday" is so important. Think about it. The hours at Mass, in catechism class, even at Catholic school could not compete with the very loud and consistent drumbeat of the messages of the world.

Even though back in the mid- to late-20th century the media weren't as prevalent as they are today, they still had an enormous impact. Television, radio, and music helped form, for example, the anti-war movement in the 1960s, along with the sexual revolution. Much of it was driven by images, songs, and media messaging, combined with the fact that many Catholic families left faith formation up to the parish and the school. It wasn't directly reinforced or discussed at length at home, and pretty soon that paved the way for the louder voices to take hold. Family faith activities were limited to grace before meals and Mass once a week.

Fast forward fifty-plus years and holy osmosis has left a good portion of the Church in a comatose state. We did all the right "Catholic" things, but we didn't really learn much.

The Cure

Like anything else that is important to us, faith takes time and effort. When we love someone, we put a lot of time and effort into that relationship. We make time for that person, and we want to learn as much as we can about them.

Getting back to the basics in terms of committing or recommitting our lives to Christ is the cure for holy osmosis. That means asking God to come into (or back into) our lives and then showing him we're serious about the relationship. We can spend more time in prayer, make an effort to read Scripture, and learn more about Catholic teachings.

Christeritis

Christeritis (pronounced "Chreester-itis") is a term my spiritual director, Monsignor Michael Bugarin, at a parish in the Archdiocese of Detroit, uses to describe people who only get to church on Christmas and Easter. After graduating from college and moving back home, I started to go back to Mass somewhat regularly to appease my parents. Dominick and I also wanted to get married in the Catholic Church. Even though we were not very active in our faith, a Catholic wedding was important to us, at least from a traditional perspective. And so, once we were engaged, we went to Mass together as a couple.

Things began to change after our wedding, and we found ourselves coming down with Christeritis early on in our marriage. It happened gradually. We were busy yuppies, and little by little we found that there were other things we had to check off our weekend to-do list. Pretty soon we were only making it to church on very special occasions. Since our understanding of God was based more on rules than relationship, the rules didn't have much meaning or staying power in our lives, and one of the big ones — the moral obligation of going to Mass once a week and keeping the Sabbath holy — just didn't seem to be that big of a deal.

Unfortunately, a large percentage of Americans who identify themselves as Catholics also believe that failure to attend Mass each week is no longer a serious sin. As mentioned earlier, only about 24 percent of Catholics in this country fulfill their weekly Mass obligation. Even if someone is still going to Mass regularly or semi-regularly, not being more involved or connected to their faith makes them more susceptible to catching a case of Christeritis from time to time, or suffering a more serious ailment that lingers for years. It's very much like not taking care of ourselves physically. Our system becomes worn down, and we're vulnerable to all kinds of germs and bugs.

Of course, we have lots of reasons for missing Mass on some (or most) Sundays. Many of us have deep-seated wounds and fears that keep us away from the Church. Over the years, I've spoken with many Catholics who are staying away, or have stayed away, from the Church because of struggles with something in their past: something they thought was so sinful that God couldn't forgive them, or that they couldn't forgive themselves, or both. I know many divorced men and women who were wrongly told by someone, somewhere, along the way, that the divorced could not receive Holy Communion, so they avoided the Church altogether. The Church teaches that the divorced certainly can receive the Eucharist as long as they are in a state of grace, meaning that they are not living in a state of mortal sin — the same requirement for all Catholics wishing to receive the Eucharist.

And then there are those men and women touched by an abortion. The statistics show that, given the number of abortions in our country (over 57 million since its legalization in 1973), one in four women in the pews has had at least one abortion. The research reveals that in addition to the women who have actually had abortions, men and many others are also somehow connected and impacted. There is, however, nothing in our past that can keep us from God. And once we confess our sins through the Sacrament of Penance and Reconciliation, we can once again receive Communion and be welcomed home. Ministries such as Rachel's Vineyard and the Silent No More Awareness Campaign, both listed in the Beyond Sunday Resource List in the appendix of this book, also help those impacted by abortion to find healing.

A few Sundays before the Easter and Christmas holidays arrive, Monsignor Bugarin does something quite wonderful, centered around this all-too-familiar malady. He doesn't criticize or condemn the "Christers." Instead, he turns to the folks in the pews:

> They're coming. You know who I'm talking about. The Christers are coming. We only see them about twice a year. They will come to church. They will take your coveted parking space and your coveted seat. They will also have a grand time eating your doughnuts and drinking your coffee. Let them. Welcome them. See this as an opportunity to evangelize and to remind them that they're welcome in this church any time and not just on the holidays.

But that's not all Monsignor does. Come the actual holiday Mass, before the recessional hymn, he tells all the Christers that he is glad to see them. He invites them to the coffee-and-doughnut social after Easter Sunday Mass, or the wine-and-cheese reception after the Easter Vigil. He lovingly suggests that they pick up a copy of the bulletin to learn about the activities going on in the parish. He reminds them that God loves them and that the Church is always their home. He is also a whiz at technology and takes full advantage of ways to reach out to parishioners who only come a couple of times a year, including robocalls to everyone and anyone still listed in the parish registry.

Being a former Christer myself, this always moves me to tears. No one is rejected, and even those who've drifted away are always welcomed back home. If this recovered Christer can return, trust me, anybody can.

The Cure

If you're already meeting your obligation of weekly Mass attendance, you're off to a great start. But to prevent a case of Christeritis from taking hold, some good insurance would be similar to the cure for Holy Osmosis: spending more time with God outside of church. The more you get to know him, the more you will want to be with him.

We've already mentioned prayer and Scripture study. Another idea would be to learn about the lives of the saints. I know that growing up Catholic I often put and kept the saints in a box or, at best, at a distance. Their statues and images were nice to look at, but they almost always seemed untouchable, not people to whom I could relate. When I actually started to read about saints, I was amazed at how much we all have in common with them. Sure, in order to be officially declared a saint by the Catholic Church, you have to have made some pretty heroic efforts for God. But saints don't start out that way. As you'll learn in the next chapter, some of our greatest saints began their incredible faith journey one effort at a time, with more than a few missteps along the way. So, pick a saint you've heard about or admired and learn more about him or her. Find out how your saint put faith into action and lived that faith beyond Sunday.

Only-on-Sunday Syndrome

Only-on-Sunday Syndrome is in many ways a strain or a virus that stems from a bad case of Holy Osmosis. We can become complacent and comfortable, thinking that we're just fine because we're checking the box each week. We put our tokens into God's slot machine, pull the handle, and expect that everything will be just fine. But if we're not careful, Only-on-Sunday Syndrome can devolve into Christeritis, because we're not going to find and fall in love with God just by going through the motions or punching a clock.

This is not to diminish the importance and the necessity of Mass and the sacraments, but the grace of the sacraments needs to be activated and cultivated through a sincere commitment to Jesus in our hearts. And that can't happen if we limit our faith to one hour every Sunday.

The Cure

"Go in peace, glorifying the Lord by your life."[4]

If you are a regular Mass attendee, you've probably heard these words before. It means exactly what this book is hopefully explaining: the necessity of going beyond Sunday.

One way to glorify God is actually learning and understanding more deeply what we do on Sunday. In several of his weekly General Audience messages during Advent 2017, Pope Francis emphasized the importance of understanding what happens at the Mass. It was part of a teaching series concerning Mass and the Eucharist. The pope's words really hit home with me. It brought me back to all the times when I have taken the Mass for granted by merely go through the motions:

> We Christians need to participate in Sunday Mass because only with the grace of Jesus, with his living presence in us and

among us, can we put into practice his commandment, and thus be his credible witnesses.

And, earlier in his message, the Holy Father said this:

Without Christ we are condemned to be dominated by the fatigue of everyday life, with its worries, and by the fear of tomorrow. The Sunday meeting with the Lord gives us the strength to live today with trust and courage and to move forward with hope.[5]

Did you ever stop and think, for example, why the Mass begins with the Sign of the Cross? In another General Audience, Pope Francis explained that it reminds us of our baptism and more:

When we make the sign of the Cross, therefore, we not only commemorate our Baptism, but affirm that the liturgical prayer is the encounter with God in Jesus Christ, who became flesh, died on the Cross and rose in glory for us.

How many Catholics know the significance of the priest bowing and kissing the altar at the beginning of Mass? The pope went on to explain that the altar is a *figure of Christ*:

These gestures, which could pass unobserved, are highly significant, because they express from the very beginning that the Mass is an encounter of love with Christ, who, by offering his Body on the Cross, became "the Priest, the Altar and the Lamb" (cf. Preface V of Easter).[6]

These are just some highlights from the pope's beautiful teaching on the Mass. I encourage you to read his reflections and any other material you can find on the Sacrifice of the Mass. If we understand the Mass more fully, we will be able to take what we see and hear into our daily lives. It will mean something more than just, as the pope pointed out, to arrive and look at the clock to make sure we're in time for the sermon.

A simple way to start living this message is to plan to get to Mass on time. The pope stresses that "it is important to make sure you do not arrive late, but rather early, in order to prepare the heart for this rite, for this community celebration."[7]

So before heading to Mass again, I encourage you to spend a few minutes with the readings ahead of time, and then get to Mass a few minutes early to settle your mind and open your heart to what God has in store. Ask God to help you apply what you're receiving to your daily life.

Chronic Catholic Curmudgeonitis

This illness is easily diagnosed, because the sufferers wear their misery on their sleeves, their faces, and everywhere else on their anatomy. The sufferers are also known to their fellow parishioners as Mr. or Mrs. Grumpy Pants. No one, except them, of course, is Catholic enough or holy enough. And unfortunately, this illness is chronic — and it's contagious.

Many of us have been affected by someone with this syndrome. It's also a reason why a lot of us stay away or don't allow ourselves to go a little deeper into our faith. Who wants to be around "pickled-peppered Christians"? This is a term Pope Francis used during one of his first homilies, at the beginning of his pontificate, to refer to Christians who aren't joyful. After all, if the joy of the Lord is truly our strength, as Scripture tells us, then why the sour face?

Our first instinct might be to ignore those who suffer from Catholic Curmudgeonitis, to run in the other direction as quickly as possible. Instead, the first thing we should do is pray for them. We should pray that God will soften their hearts and help them see the good around them. Not that we should be burying our heads in the sand when it comes to issues in the world or the Church that need to be addressed. But we can pray that these folks can regain a sense of hope and joy — the joy that will help them develop a positive attitude that could help reverse some of what they see going wrong with the Church or the parish.

Second, we need to recognize that, deep down, the frustrations come from an actual deep love of God and a deep concern for the state of the Church. Many of their concerns may often be justified, but concentrating on the negative too much can immobilize a person to the point where the only activity in which they are involved is promoting more negativity. Yet it's important for us to understand that, at some level, their heart is in the right place. Perhaps you could be just the person to encourage them by asking them what they can do, or what you can do together with them, to make a difference starting at the parish level.

Maybe you can take a closer look at the parish bulletin and see where help is needed within a particular ministry. Maybe you can encourage the Grumpy Pants family, as well as your own circle of family and friends, to check out that Bible study or prayer group meeting that's mentioned in a recent bulletin post or article. Doing good and growing in understanding of the Faith are two surefire ways to cure Catholic Curmudgeonitis. It's hard to be grumpy when you're around people excited about their faith or volunteering for a worthy cause.

Third, never let anyone steal your joy. In a homily, Pope Francis has reminded us to share our joy with others and not to keep it to ourselves:

> If we keep this joy to ourselves it will make us sick in the end, our hearts will grow old and wrinkled and our faces will no longer transmit that great joy, only nostalgia and melancholy which is not healthy.

We need to remember what true joy is. It's not a matter of financial security, for example, or the idea that everything in life has to be fun or exciting. It goes much deeper than that. Pope Francis went on to say:

> Joy is a gift from God. It fills us from within.... Joy cannot be held at heel: it must be let go. Joy is a pilgrim virtue. It is a gift that walks, walks on the path of life that walks with Jesus: preaching, proclaiming Jesus, proclaiming joy, lengthens and widens that path. It is a virtue of the Great, of those Great ones who rise above the little things in life, above human pettiness, of those who will not allow themselves to be dragged into those little things within the community, within the Church: they always look to the horizon.[8]

It's also a good idea to take some time to think about how we might be catching our own case of Catholic Curmudgeonitis. My husband and I had to face this reality shortly after we came back to the Church. We were so excited about our faith. We were learning new things almost every single day. And pretty soon we started to wonder why, after growing up in the Faith, we hadn't heard any of this before. (At least, that's what it felt like.) Sometimes we allowed that question to take over and would get very frustrated, very quickly, if we thought Father So-and-So or Bishop So-and-So wasn't strong enough or direct enough in their teaching. We complained and whined a lot but never bothered to ask what we could do to help improve the situation. After all, wasn't that *their* job?

At speaking engagements and through my radio show, I hear from many Catholics who express similar frustrations. Archbishop Vigneron warns of what can happen when we allow this ailment to get the best of us. It doesn't do us or the Church any good. The archbishop writes:

> A common temptation in reaction to problems is to lament that we no longer have the power or prestige we once had. We don't have as many priests, as many resources, as much money, as much support. Like the Israelites in the desert, we can take on an attitude of "murmuring," finding fault with God and others. But complaining leads only to discouragement and paralysis. God thinks we have enough, because we have him. "I can do all things in him who strengthens me" (Phil 4:13).[9]

It took time for Dominick and me to learn how to turn our frustrations into positive motivation. It took time for us to understand what we could and couldn't change. Certainly, there are problems in the Catholic Church. If there weren't, there would be no need to write this book. Nor would my archbishop, along with other leaders in the Church, feel compelled to highlight and address some of these crucial issues. But the best way to address the problems is to be part of the solutions.

Listeners to my radio show write to me all the time complaining that there is not enough being done in their diocese about this, that, or the other thing. But when I ask them what they're doing about a particular issue, they either fall silent or claim it's the priest's or deacon's responsibility. Granted, if we're talking about a hierarchical issue, or an issue pertaining to the sacramental life of the Church, yes, it is the responsibility of the clergy. But a majority of the problems in the Church can be traced back to the title of this book. Not enough of us are "beyond Sunday" Catholics, due primarily to a lack of evangelization. And because we are all called to evangelize by virtue of our baptism, a big chunk of the responsibility is also ours. No room for Chronic Catholic Curmudgeonitis or Mr. and Mrs. Grumpy Pants here. We need to turn that frown upside down and get busy.

The Cure

Whether we suffer from Chronic Catholic Curmudgeonitis ourselves or have been hurt by people in the pews around us who suffer from this disease, the cure is basically the same. We need to discover, develop, and use our gifts to help fulfill the Church's mission. In 2012, Pope Benedict XVI called for this in his message to the Catholic Action forum, "Ecclesial and Social Co-Responsibility":

> Never tire of increasingly refining the aspects of your specific vocation as lay faithful called to be courageous and credible witnesses in all social milieus so that the Gospel may be a light that brings hope to the problematic, difficult and dark situations which people today often encounter in their journey through life.[10]

How might God be calling you to spread the light of the Gospel in his Church? Once we figure that out and start living it, Chronic Catholic Curmudgeonitis has no more room to spread.

Even in the face of the worst chronic Catholic ailment, we can have peace and confidence that there is a cure, because Jesus is the great physician. If we ask him — and invite him into our lives to do it — he will cure what ails us all … and then some.

MONDAY

Reflect: Which of these common Catholic ailments might be afflicting you?

TUESDAY

Read: "The Roots of the Crisis," section 3.3 (beginning on page 12) of Archbishop Vigneron's letter *Unleash the Gospel*, available at www.unleashthegospel.org. This will give you some additional food for thought, not only for your own "beyond Sunday" journey, but it will also provide insight on how you can help others close to you who may be having similar experiences.

WEDNESDAY

Reflect: As you continue your "beyond Sunday" journey this week, what new insights have you gained about yourself and the Church that might be leading to a cure for your common Catholic ailment?

THURSDAY

Pray: Ask God to show you the steps you need to take to leave that common Catholic ailment behind.

FRIDAY

Read: "Good and Bad Habits," section 3.4 (beginning on page 14) of *Unleash the Gospel*. Pick one good habit to put into practice, which will help you cure your common Catholic ailment.

SATURDAY

Read & Reflect: Read and reflect on the readings for this Sunday, which you can find at www.usccb.org/bible/readings.

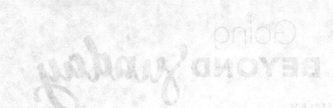
Going
BEYOND Sunday

MONDAY

Reflect. Which of these common Catholic ailments might be afflicting you?

TUESDAY

Read. The Rocks of the Cracle, section 33 (beginning on page 127 of Archbishop Vigneron's letter Unleash the Gospel, available at www.unleashthegospel.org). This will give you some additional food for thought, not only for your own Beyond Sunday journey, but it will also provide insight on how you can help others close to you who may be having similar experiences.

WEDNESDAY

Reflect. As you continue your "beyond Sunday" journey this week, what new insights have you gained about yourself and the Church that might be leading to a cure for your common Catholic ailment?

THURSDAY

Pray. Ask God to show you the steps you need to take to leave that common Catholic ailment behind.

FRIDAY

Read. "Good and Bad Failure," section 3.11 (beginning on page 127 through the end). Pick one good habit to put into practice which will help you cure your common Catholic ailment.

SATURDAY

Read & Reflect. Read and reflect on the readings for this Sunday, which you can find at www.usccb.org/bible/readings.

CHAPTER THREE

"Late Have I Loved You"

We're Not the Only Ones Taking the Long Way Home

....

"Late have I loved you, Beauty so ancient and so new."
— SAINT AUGUSTINE OF HIPPO

One of the most common reasons many of us can't take faith not only beyond Sunday but to church in the first place is that deep down we just don't see ourselves as lovable. Whether it's painful relationships in our lives or some pretty stinky stuff in the past, we don't believe we would be, or could be, welcomed into the parish parking lot, let alone in the pews. We're convinced that we've been away too long, and that it's simply too late.

Whether you're reading this book because you have been struggling in your own faith walk, or to help a friend or a relative who has fallen away from the Church, know this: you are lovable, and you belong in the Church, no matter what you may have done or how far you may have wandered in your life. As I said earlier, the Church is a field hospital for sinners. And it always has been.

We continue this journey of going beyond Sunday by going back in Church history to examine the incredible lives of some of those giants who've gone before us. Maybe you get intimidated when looking at some of the great saints. Instead, we should be encouraged and inspired because, as surprising as it might seem, their lives show us that we are hardly alone when it comes to the questioning, the wondering, and the searching. Or you might be wondering, as I did many times, what in the world a bunch of holier-than-thou dead folks have to do with you and your spiritual life (or the lack thereof) in the thoroughly modern world? The answer: a lot more than you might suspect.

First of all, the saints are not dead. If we call ourselves Christians, we believe the journey here on earth is only the beginning of life. The goal is to be reunited with God in heaven, and that's where the saints are, a lot more fully alive than any of us. Scripture beautifully describes the saints in heaven as a "cloud of witnesses": "Therefore, since we are surrounded by so great a cloud of witnesses, let us also lay aside every weight, and sin which clings so closely, and let us run with perseverance the race that is set before us" (Heb 12:1).

Second, according to the Bible and the *Catechism of the Catholic Church*, the heavenly souls intercede for us day in and day out. The *Catechism* assures us:

> "[The saints] do not cease to intercede with the Father for us, as they proffer the merits which they acquired on earth through the one mediator between God and men, Christ Jesus.... So by their fraternal concern is our weakness greatly helped" (*LG* 49; cf. 1 Tim 2:5). (CCC 956)

For most of my life, I kept the saints quite literally on a shelf. When I was growing up in a very Catholic and very Italian American home, religious images were quite common. Statues of Saint Anthony and Saint Francis were especially popular, along with Saint Lawrence, who is the patron saint of cooks. But it wasn't until much later in my life that I really got to know any of them outside of the holy cards my great-aunts and grandmothers collected, or the old faded religious paintings that hung on the wall. This is not to minimize or poke fun at the importance of keeping sacred images in the home. It would be pretty hypocritical of me to downplay the practice, since my office now resembles a religious bookstore. God really does have a sense of humor.

When I did begin to study the lives of the saints, I was surprised — well, more like relieved — that many of them were not always holy. Far from it. They struggled, they questioned, and, yes, they sinned — some of them in big ways. It was a long time before quite a few of our saints found their way back home.

"There is hope for me yet," I thought. There is hope for all of us, even those of us who still feel far from where we need to be in our relationship with, or understanding of, God.

Saint Augustine of Hippo (354–430)

Saint Augustine of Hippo is just the right man to help us in our enlightened modern age, when many consider themselves too intelligent for Christianity. This is one of the big challenges facing Catholics and other Christians today, and it's not so different from challenges faced by the early Christians. As it says in the Old Testament Book of Ecclesiastes, "There is nothing new under the sun" (1:9). Christians are often called ignorant or weak — or both. If we're not well grounded in our beliefs and lack a basic understanding of Scripture and the Gospel message, we're easy pickings and can be quickly led astray, left with a great deal of doubt.

Although raised by a Christian mother, Augustine spent a good portion of his life dabbling in philosophical ideologies and religions that appealed more to his intellect. He was born in the fourth century and received a Christian education thanks to his devout mother, Monica (who also became a great saint). His early associations with faithful people exposed him to Jesus, but due to the moral crisis that was swirling around him at the time, as well as his own weaknesses, he kept faith at a distance for many years. Augustine excelled in school, but he spent years trying to find a philosophy he could adhere to without needing to embrace faith. He became heavily involved in the heretical teachings of Manichaeism, a religion founded by Mani, a Persian, in the third century. It claimed to contain the truths or synthesis of all religions, bringing salvation by knowledge.

As a young man, Augustine began a long-term, live-in relationship with a woman and fathered a child out of wedlock. None of this is exactly the kind of behavior one would expect from a future bishop — and not just any bishop, but one of the greatest Christian teachers to walk the earth. He not only became a saint, but was given the title Doctor of the Church, a title bestowed on those who distinguish themselves by their orthodoxy and body of teaching.

So how did this wild child and Mr. Know-It-All eventually have a huge "come to Jesus" moment? Well, to make a long and amazing story short, Augustine was frustrated by a number of things, including the unhappiness he felt from his lifestyle. Despite his success as a teacher and orator, he often felt lost and ashamed of many of his choices. His search for truth had led him to a lot of dead ends. Finally, through the prayers and the efforts of his mother, he came to know Saint Ambrose, the bishop of Milan. Augustine was impressed by Ambrose's teaching and preaching, and he was eventually convinced that Christianity was the one true faith.

As Augustine explained years later in one of the most well-known and beloved excerpts from his famous autobiography, *The Confessions*:

> Late have I loved you, Beauty so ancient and so new, late have I loved you. Lo, you were within, but I outside seeking there for you and upon the shapely things you have made I rushed headlong, I, misshapen. You were with me but I was not with you.

Saint Francis of Assisi (1182–1226)

Even if you don't know much about the life of Saint Francis of Assisi, you're familiar with him. He can be found in many a garden or backyard because of his association with, and love of, nature. He is the patron saint of animals and ecology. Unfortunately, he is often viewed, and even described by some, as a holy zookeeper or a medieval Dr. Dolittle, someone who never had a care or a challenge in the world: a simple, jolly monk who spent his days dancing through the tulips and sunflowers, talking to the animals.

But Saint Francis himself tells quite a different story about his faith journey, and some of the details aren't pretty. In his own words: "I have been all things unholy. If God can work through me, he can work through anyone."

For a while, Francis was indeed the bad boy of Assisi, Italy, living a life of luxury and getting into trouble. By his own admission, he was a party animal and indulged in all kinds of fancy foods, wines, and — well — lots of partying. He was known to break the city curfew more than once and didn't actually start to settle down and reflect upon his life until he was thrown into prison following a battle between Assisi and Perugia. Since his family was quite wealthy, he was held for ransom.

While waiting for his father to pay for his freedom, Francis came down with a fever that got him started thinking about eternity. Upon his release, he tried to join another army headed off to battle, but he heard God telling him to return home. Soon after that, Francis had a dream in which Christ asked him to rebuild the Church.

(If you ever get the opportunity to visit Assisi, you'll see this saint's fascinating story, told through breathtaking frescoes on the walls of the basilica named after him. Pilgrims spend hours gazing at the scenes showing the stunning turnaround of another wild child.)

Francis was so convinced of his need to leave his footloose and fancy-free existence that he wanted to make sure his intentions to leave the world behind and follow Christ would be clearly understood. Quite dramatically, in the middle of town, in front of his father (who wasn't exactly thrilled with his son's newfound faith) and the bishop, he tore off his fancy clothes and left them right there on the ground for all to see. How's that for a grand exit from the lifestyles of the rich and famous?

The rest, as they say, is history. Saint Francis and his love for the Lord and the simple life attracted many men and women over the centuries, enabling the religious order he founded (the Franciscans) to grow and thrive. He is one of the Catholic Church's most beloved saints. And, like Augustine, he made a huge mark on the Church.

"The Greater the Sin, the Greater the Mercy"

Given that there are more than ten thousand saints in the Catholic Church, there are plenty of other dramatic U-turn tales to be told. The moral of their stories is this: everybody has something. I have heard it said (I am not sure by whom), "Every saint has a past; every sinner has a future." But sometimes our doubts or our guilt from previous mistakes keep us away from God. We think, "There is no way God can forgive me." Maybe it is something in our past. Maybe it is a negative image implanted in our heads early on, of God as some mean ogre in the sky, waiting to punish us. We're stuck with a very distorted picture of him, which blocks us from taking full advantage of his never-ending mercy.

That's why Pope Francis declared a Year of Mercy in the Catholic Church, which began on the feast of the Immaculate Conception, December 8, 2015, and concluded on the feast of Christ the King, November 20, 2016. In his Year of Mercy letter, the pope told the Church and the world that he wanted the year to be a true experience of the mercy of God. He stated in his message that no one is too far gone

to receive God's forgiveness and mercy. Did you catch that? *No one* —
and he exemplified this by highlighting those whom society often casts
aside as hopeless causes: those behind bars.

> My thoughts also turn to those incarcerated, whose freedom
> is limited. The Jubilee Year has always constituted an
> opportunity for great amnesty, which is intended to include
> the many people who, despite deserving punishment, have
> become conscious of the injustice they worked and sincerely
> wish to re-enter society and make their honest contribution to
> it. May they all be touched in a tangible way by the mercy of
> the Father who wants to be close to those who have the greatest
> need of his forgiveness.

Many people who are not in prison also feel far away from the
reach of God's mercy. Perhaps no one feels this more than those who
have had or assisted in abortions. In my work as a Catholic journalist, I
have had the opportunity to interview many post-abortion women and
men, and I've found many people stay away from Jesus and the Church
because they believe their sin in having or helping someone procure
an abortion is unforgivable. But in this same letter, Pope Francis had a
message for them as well:

> I think in particular of all the women who have resorted to
> abortion. I am well aware of the pressure that has led them to
> this decision. I know that it is an existential and moral ordeal.
> I have met so many women who bear in their heart the scar
> of this agonizing and painful decision. What has happened is
> profoundly unjust; yet only understanding the truth of it can
> enable one not to lose hope. The forgiveness of God cannot be
> denied to one who has repented, especially when that person
> approaches the Sacrament of Confession with a sincere heart
> in order to obtain reconciliation with the Father.[11]

Francis spoke this message of mercy throughout the special year
in all types of venues, including his weekly General Audience, which
takes place in St. Peter's Square every Wednesday morning. During
Easter week 2016, leading up to the feast of Divine Mercy, his audience
message turned into a sort of "mercy pep rally":

God is greater than our sin. Let us not forget this: God is greater than our sin! "Father, I do not know how to say it. I have committed many, serious [sins]!" God is greater than all the sins we can commit. God is greater than our sin. Shall we say it together? All together: "God is greater than our sin!" Once again: "God is greater than our sin!" Once more: "God is greater than our sin!" His love is an ocean in which we can immerse ourselves without fear of being overcome: to God forgiving means giving us the certainty that he never abandons us. Whatever our heart may admonish us, he is still and always greater than everything (cf. 1 Jn 3:20), because God is greater than our sin.

The pope went on to tell the crowds about one of the most notorious sinners in the Bible: King David. You think you have sins? If King David were alive today and ahead of you in the confession line, your clothes would change style and then some before your turn finally came.

King David was called by God to shepherd his people and guide them on "the paths of obedience to divine law." This sounded quite noble — until the king became a bit overconfident and forgot that he himself was also supposed to follow that obedience clause. David had an affair with Bathsheba, the wife of one of his military officers, and got her pregnant. Then, to cover it over, he also had Bathsheba's husband killed. Yet, despite everything, when David repented, God not only forgave him but also referred to David as a man after his own heart because he was truly sorry for his mistakes. David gave himself and God another chance.

Pope Francis had this to say, relating David's story to each of us:

God blots out our sin from the very root, completely! Therefore the penitent person becomes pure again; every stain is eliminated and now he is whiter than pure snow. We are all sinners. Is this true? If any of you does not feel you are a sinner, raise your hand.... No one. We all are sinners. We sinners, with forgiveness, become new creatures, filled by the spirit and full of joy. Now a new reality begins for us: a new heart, a new spirit, a new life. We, forgiven sinners, who have received divine grace, can even teach others to sin no more. "But Father,

I am weak, I fall, I fall" — "If you fall, get up! Stand up!" When a child falls, what does he do? He raises his hand to mom, to dad so they help him to get up. Let us do the same! If out of weakness you fall into sin, raise your hand: the Lord will take it and help you get up. This is the dignity of God's forgiveness! The dignity that God's forgiveness gives us is that of lifting us up, putting us back on our feet, because he created men and woman to stand on their feet.[12]

Saint Maria Faustina Kowalska (1905–1938)

Over the past several years, the message of mercy has received a lot of attention, thanks to the combined efforts of Pope Francis and his predecessors, Benedict XVI and Saint John Paul II. The message of Divine Mercy was entrusted to Saint Maria Faustina Kowalska, known as the Apostle of Divine Mercy. The message should be a comfort to all of us, especially to anyone feeling like a prodigal son or daughter.

Saint Faustina — a humble, simple nun from Poland — was canonized by John Paul II in 2000. Starting in the 1930s, she received powerful messages from Christ regarding the love and mercy of God. Christ asked her to record the messages, which are now contained in what's known as the *Diary of Saint Maria Faustina Kowalska*. Pope Francis summarized this message to Faustina by saying, "God is greater than our sin." Or, as C. S. Lewis expressed it, "The greater the sin, the greater the mercy."

The message of mercy itself is certainly nothing new in the Catholic Church or in Christianity in general. Yet we quickly forget it. Over the centuries, however, the Lord has raised up great saints to remind us of how much he loves us. Saint Augustine and Saint Francis are strong reminders that even those with checkered pasts can be transformed into new creations that glorify and help bring others to God.

While Saint Faustina has no scandalous backstory, she was hardly a Rhodes scholar, and she was not the type of person one might expect to have such a major influence on the Church. John Paul II, at her canonization, told the world that Saint Faustina, too, carries the message of mercy. It's a message all of us need to hear, no matter what our past looks like.

The Marian Fathers, who run the National Shrine of The Divine Mercy in Stockbridge, Massachusetts, say Christ's message of mercy, given to Saint Faustina, can be applied to our lives as simply as the letters ABC. (Sort of a Catholic version of that classic Jackson 5 tune, "A, B, C. Easy as one, two, three.")

(A) Ask for his mercy. God wants us to approach him in prayer constantly, repenting of our sins and asking him to pour his mercy out upon us and upon the whole world.

(B) Be merciful. God wants us to receive his mercy and let it flow through us to others. He wants us to extend love and forgiveness to others, just as he does to us.

(C) Completely trust in Jesus. God wants us to know that the graces of his mercy are dependent upon our trust. The more we trust in Jesus, the more we will receive.

So, what are you waiting for? It doesn't matter where you have been or where you are now. It doesn't matter how far you may feel from home. Even if you've taken the long way, you can choose today, with the help of God's grace and mercy, to start walking. Think of Saint Augustine, Saint Francis, Saint Faustina, King David, and the vast membership of the communion of saints — and remember, you're in good company.

Going BEYOND Sunday

MONDAY

Pray: Today, pray the prayer that Jesus asked Saint Faustina to have written at the bottom of the Divine Mercy image: "Jesus, I trust in you." Try to call it to mind throughout the day.

TUESDAY

Read: The story of the Prodigal Son in Luke 15:11–32. See where you see yourself and God in this parable.

WEDNESDAY

Reflect: Do you believe that God's mercy is for you too? Why or why not?

THURSDAY

Act: Read the Spiritual and Corporal Works of Mercy in the Beyond Sunday Resource List of this book, and act on one this week, such as smiling and saying "hello" to people you encounter, visiting, or calling a sick friend, etc.

FRIDAY

Act: Is there someone in your life (including yourself) who needs your mercy and/or forgiveness? How can you practice the ABC's of mercy, mentioned in this chapter, toward that person?

SATURDAY

Read & Reflect: Read and reflect on the readings for this Sunday, which you can find at www.usccb.org/bible/readings.

CHAPTER FOUR

Conscience and the American Catholic

....

"We also must learn to listen more to our conscience.
Be careful, however: this does not mean we ought to follow our ego,
do whatever interests us, whatever suits us, whatever pleases us.
That is not conscience."[13]
— POPE FRANCIS

In April 2016, the Pew Research Center released the results of an extensive survey of more than three thousand Catholics and other Christians about religion in their daily lives.[14]

I cringed as I read the results, not so much because I was greatly disappointed (though I was), but because I felt like I was looking at myself, in so much of my own life as a cradle Catholic.

According to the researchers, many Catholics who attend Mass weekly and pray regularly admitted they're not very likely to consult Scripture, Church teachings, or the writings and statements of religious leaders such as the pope when making major moral decisions.

Instead, according to the survey results, these Catholics say that they consult their "own conscience" on these decisions:

- About three-quarters of U.S. Catholics (73 percent) say they look to their own conscience "a great deal" for guidance on difficult moral questions. Far fewer Catholics say they rely a great deal on the Catholic Church's teachings (21 percent), the Bible (15 percent), or the pope (11 percent) for such guidance.

- Catholics who are highly religious are more likely than less religious Catholics to turn to Church teachings, the Bible, or the pope for guidance on difficult moral questions. Still, far fewer highly religious Catholics say they rely a great deal on any of these three sources for guidance on tough moral questions than they rely on their own conscience.

Yet, what is the conscience? Sadly, for most of us today, all we know is what Jiminy Cricket told Pinocchio in the Disney classic: "Always let your conscience be your guide." Since we don't know what our conscience really is, we assume it has something to do with our feelings and deeply held opinions or emotions that run very deep. That's where we run into trouble.

Here's the problem: in reality, conscience is not rooted in feelings, personal opinions, prayers, or occasional deep thoughts. Instead, as the online Catholic Dictionary states, conscience is the following:

The judgment of the practical intellect deciding, from general principles of faith and reason, the goodness or badness of a way of acting that a person now faces.

It is an operation of the intellect and not of the feelings or even of the will. An action is right or wrong because of objective principles to which the mind must subscribe, not because a person subjectively feels that way or because his will wants it that way.

Conscience, therefore, is a specific act of the mind applying its knowledge to a concrete moral situation. What the mind decides in a given case depends on principles already in the mind.[15]

That "knowledge" is attained by a lot more than just reading a few newspaper articles, listening to talk shows, or chatting with family and friends. This is exactly what I did for a good portion of my life, falsely believing I was being led by my "own conscience," when in reality I wasn't going very deep at all. I was not venturing beyond surface emotions and opinions, and certainly not following Church teaching.

I can also honestly say there was little or no prayer involved and no consultation with those knowledgeable in the faith.

It's really quite ironic. Well, "shocking" might be a better word for it, especially for someone trained as a journalist, as I was, who was very good at research and digging deeper when it came to covering an important story. But when it came to making serious moral decisions in my life, all of that training was never applied. I just did what I felt was right at the time for me.

Today, when we have so much information quite literally at our fingertips, we have no excuse for claiming ignorance about what the Church teaches when it comes to serious moral matters. It's not all that difficult to find out what the Church teaches on any given topic, and yet how many of us bother to go beyond the headlines of a few sensational articles about what the pope said or did, to seek real knowledge about our faith?

Now don't get me wrong. The Church doesn't tell us that we can't read or watch the news, or listen to our favorite talk show in order to help us gather information. But the Church does tell us that such sources are only the beginning. When it comes to forming our conscience properly as Catholic Christians, everything needs to be done in light of our relationship with God. If we're serious about that relationship, we will take that formation to God in prayer, as Pope Francis reminded us in an Angelus address several years ago:

> Conscience is the interior space in which we can listen to and hear the truth, the good, the voice of God. It is the inner place of our relationship with him, who speaks to our heart and helps us to discern, to understand the path we ought to take, and once the decision is made, to move forward, to remain faithful.[16]

Forming Our Conscience

An email conversation I had with a listener of mine is, I think, an example of an unhealthy pattern that many Catholics, myself included, adopted at one time or another when it comes to forming our conscience.

The listener sent her original email in response to one of many discussions I had on Catholics voting their conscience. This woman was writing to explain that she was about to cast her vote for several politicians locally and nationally who supported activities and issues in direct opposition to core Church teaching. But, she explained, she was fine with her decision because she had done some reading, she prayed about it, and "consulted her conscience."

I wrote her back and asked her what type of sources she had consulted, in addition to the secular news sources she mentioned. She referred to herself as a well-educated Catholic, a product of Catholic schools, and efficient at research. Had she consulted the *Catechism of the Catholic Church*? Did she talk with a priest or someone who had a good understanding of a Catholic's responsibility when voting? Did she review any of the bishops' documents on voting and proper faith formation? Did she spend more than just a few minutes in prayer before making those decisions?

She was kind and honest enough to write back and explain that the answer to all of the questions I raised was a flat-out "no." She didn't consult any Catholic sources at all, only secular news sources, along with websites and other links directly connected to her political party of preference. She also didn't own a copy of the *Catechism* and never even thought about speaking with anyone other than her husband and a few close friends, all of whom, by her own admission, knew little about their faith. I admire her courage in admitting that she hadn't really spent much time in prayer and obviously still had some work to do.

Something else I shared with this listener, since she was open to what I had to say, was concerning reliance on the secular media for information on faith-based issues — or, really, relying on the secular media for information on any major issue nowadays. (As someone who spent half of her professional life in secular newsrooms, I can tell you that this is a mistake.) The media, in general, have become very sloppy and very much agenda driven; and their agenda is hardly in line with Catholic values.

Studies going as far back as the early 1980s show that a majority of those who work inside America's newsrooms are either agnostic or atheist. A majority also strongly support legalized abortion on demand, so-called same-sex marriage, and artificial contraception, just to name a few of the hot-button issues. In a perfect world, their personal opinions shouldn't matter. Journalists should be able to cover stories by at least attempting to report on both sides without revealing what they believe or feel. But those days, for the most part, are long gone. The studies confirming liberal media bias are too many to list here. Religion isn't important to them unless it's an opportunity to criticize religion — in particular, the core teachings of the Catholic Church, beliefs also shared by evangelicals and other people of faith. Some in the media industry admit as much, saying they just don't "get religion."

In an interview one month after the 2016 presidential election, Dean Baquet, the executive editor of *The New York Times*, told the *Business Insider* that the media not only don't understand religion but also don't recognize the important role it still plays in the lives of many Americans:

> I think that the New York-based — and Washington-based too, probably — media powerhouses don't quite get religion. We have a fabulous religion writer, but she's all alone. We don't get religion. We don't get the role of religion in people's lives. And I think we can do much, much better.[17]

The fact that a major publication such as *The New York Times* has only one religion writer should be a strong indication of how little emphasis the media place on the topic. At the same time, matters relating to religion and faith are consistently in the news, and that should be a motivation for us to be willing to look at what the Church has to say, instead of turning to the secular news as a major source when it comes to forming our conscience.

One reason many Catholics, such as the radio listener previously mentioned, do not consult Catholic sources is they don't even know that there are such Catholic sources, including great documents by the popes and bishops, which are there to guide us in living and making decisions based on our faith. Greg Erlandson, director and editor in chief of Catholic News Service, a Catholic newswire, says this is still all too common in the Church today:

> Unfortunately, most Catholics today rely on secular media for their information about the Church. Not only does this mean they get a sparse and selective coverage of Church news, too often they get nothing at all. If a bishop issues a statement, in other words, and no one hears it, did it exist?[18]

Speaking of statements or documents, Erlandson also encourages Catholics to take a close look at Cardinal John Foley's 1992 pastoral instruction on social communications, *Aetatis Novae*, which highlighted this very issue so clearly:

> The power of media extends to defining not only what people will think but even what they will think about. Reality, for many, is what the media recognize as real; what media do not acknowledge seems of little importance. Thus de facto silence can be imposed upon individuals and groups whom the media ignore; and even the voice of the Gospel can be muted, though not entirely stilled, in this way.[19]

Certainly, we're all busy. It can be a bit overwhelming to think about carving out more time in our already jampacked day, to add one more thing to that ever-growing to-do list. But when something is important to us, we do take the time. We find the time for the things and people we love. We find the time and do the research, the thinking, and the analyzing when it comes to other big decisions. If we're buying a new home, we are going to seek out a real estate agent with experience and knowledge of the neighborhoods we're considering. We're going to talk with people who live in those neighborhoods. We're going to take our time finding the best schools in those neighborhoods and talk to administrators, teachers, even other parents. We're going to do our homework.

And that's what properly forming our conscience entails. It involves doing our spiritual homework. When we were growing up, it was our parents and other authoritative figures that helped us in our formation process. As children, we are given discipline and structure. At times, looking back, we can think that the discipline, structure, or rules were all fine when we were young; but as adults, we're smart enough to make a go of it on our own. This is the approach I took, and it's the same approach the listener mentioned earlier took. We consider this true freedom, having the ability to make up our own minds. Yet Pope Francis has explained that true freedom comes in being open to God and what he is trying to say to us, as opposed to silencing that inner voice:

> Jesus wants us free, and this freedom — where is it found? It is to be found in the inner dialogue with God in conscience. If a Christian does not know how to talk with God, does not know

how to listen to God, in his own conscience, then he is not free — he is not free.[20]

The *Catechism* also clearly states that formation of conscience, just like our relationship with Jesus, is a lifelong commitment:

> The education of the conscience is a lifelong task. From the earliest years, it awakens the child to the knowledge and practice of the interior law recognized by conscience. Prudent education teaches virtue; it prevents or cures fear, selfishness and pride, resentment arising from guilt, and feelings of complacency, born of human weakness and faults. The education of the conscience guarantees freedom and engenders peace of heart.
>
> In the formation of conscience, the Word of God is the light for our path (cf. Ps 119:105), we must assimilate it in faith and prayer and put it into practice. We must also examine our conscience before the Lord's Cross. We are assisted by the gifts of the Holy Spirit, aided by the witness or advice of others and guided by the authoritative teaching of the Church. (CCC 1784–1785)

If we break down the last part of this *Catechism* quote, we can see the step-by-step process we should take in forming our conscience:

- We should take a look at what the Bible has to say about the decisions we're trying to make.
- We should pray about our decisions earnestly.
- We should ask for help from the Holy Spirit.
- We should turn toward those knowledgeable in the Faith — perhaps our pastor or someone involved in teaching the Faith.
- And last, but not least, we should use the teachings of the Church as our guide. If we come to a decision that is directly in conflict with what our faith teaches, then we need to go back to the spiritual drawing board.

Moral Relativism

Something that's become all too common, even among some in the Church, is the idea or concept of "moral relativism." This is the idea that there is no objective truth or reality. Whatever a person believes is fine, and it's judgmental, offensive, even harmful to suggest otherwise. On the surface, at first this may sound fair. But, in actuality, it's a lie and a major obstruction when it comes to living a moral life and properly forming our conscience.

In fact, we only need to begin to scratch the surface ever so slightly to see how this way of thinking is really not good at all. It's not really even thinking. What happens when personal views or opinions collide, or when our egos, as Pope Francis mentioned, get in the way? Which view wins? Who determines what's legislated and what isn't? How does that pan out in a civilized society? And if all are free to believe what they want, then anything goes. Out goes morality, and in comes chaos. Even worse, everyone is actually not free to believe as he or she wishes, as we are seeing in our society now. The next progression is what we're seeing in our culture: an outright hostility toward people of faith who are trying to live out that faith in their everyday lives. Think about all the lawsuits involving the butcher, the baker, and the candlestick maker, as of late, for their refusal to go against their religious beliefs.

Supposedly, it's all about tolerance, when in reality, as Cardinal Joseph Ratzinger said in his 2005 homily before the papal conclave, it really results in having just the opposite effect:

> Today, having a clear faith based on the Creed of the Church is often labeled as fundamentalism. Whereas relativism, that is, letting oneself be "tossed here and there, carried about by every wind of doctrine," seems the only attitude that can cope with modern times. We are building a dictatorship of relativism that does not recognize anything as definitive and whose ultimate goal consists solely of one's own ego and desires.

Sound familiar? These words, spoken, in April 2005, by the soon-to-be new Pope Benedict XVI, are very similar to the words spoken by Pope Francis, in 2013, warning us of wrongly thinking that following our conscience means anything goes.

To combat this error and avoid the trap of relativism, Cardinal Ratzinger reminded us that we need to have an adult faith, not a faith that goes with the flow of the current trends:

> We, however, have a different goal: the Son of God, the true man. He is the measure of true humanism. An "adult" faith

is not a faith that follows the trends of fashion and the latest novelty; a mature adult faith is deeply rooted in friendship with Christ. It is this friendship that opens us up to all that is good and gives us a criterion by which to distinguish the true from the false, and deceit from truth.

We must develop this adult faith; we must guide the flock of Christ to this faith. And it is this faith — only faith — that creates unity and is fulfilled in love.

Moral relativism leads to confusion, whereas our Catholic faith, including the formation of one's conscience, is always about leading us through love to the truth, as Cardinal Ratzinger explained:

> On this theme, St. Paul offers us as a fundamental formula for Christian existence some beautiful words, in contrast to the continual vicissitudes of those who, like children, are tossed about by the waves: make truth in love. Truth and love coincide in Christ. To the extent that we draw close to Christ, in our own lives too, truth and love are blended. Love without truth would be blind; truth without love would be like "a clanging cymbal" (1 Cor 13:1).[21]

One important exercise Catholics are encouraged to do every day to form their conscience is called an "examination of conscience." This entails looking at our actions, words, thoughts, and the good things we've failed to do, in light of the Ten Commandments and the teachings of the Church. It requires a lot of honesty and a good dose of humility, but the benefits of performing this exercise every day are truly life-changing.

If we're still breathing, God isn't done with us yet, and there is work to be done in growing and learning about the Lord and the Church he founded. God is supposed to be first in our lives. His word and the teachings of the Church are not mere suggestions: they are real commands, meant to govern our lives. The Ten Commandments and the teachings of the Church, combined with the help of the Holy Spirit, all aid in the formation of our conscience and lead us into a faithful life.

Going BEYOND Sunday

MONDAY

Pray: Ask God to show you if there are any areas in your life where you are making up your own rules instead of following his.

TUESDAY

Read: Today open your Bible and read Exodus 20:1–17 (or Deuteronomy 5:6–21). These are the Ten Commandments God gave us, and it's important that we recognize they are not the "Ten Suggestions." These commands of God actually bring us freedom, not restraint, when we make them part of our lives. Do you believe that?

WEDNESDAY

Pray: Ask God to help you form and strengthen your conscience correctly, according to his commandments, the teachings of his Church, and the Holy Spirit's loving guidance.

THURSDAY

Reflect: Having a proper understanding of a well-formed conscience guides Catholics beyond Sunday into a powerful relationship with God and the Church. Do you believe that following God's laws can truly lead to lasting peace and fulfillment? What is holding you back from believing this fully?

FRIDAY

Act: Do an examination of conscience and plan to attend confession tomorrow. Most parishes hold confessions before the Vigil Mass on Saturday afternoons.

SATURDAY

Challenge: Whether it's been months or years, encounter God's mercy today in confession (or, more formally, the Sacrament of Penance and Reconciliation) today. Remember, no sin is unforgivable, and Jesus is ready, with open arms, to embrace you with his mercy.

CHAPTER FIVE

Up Close and Personal
The Church and God in Our Everyday Lives

If I am delayed, you may know how one ought to behave
in the household of God, which is the Church of the living God, the
pillar and bulwark of the truth.
— 1 TIMOTHY 3:15

God has given us the Church as a gift, because he loves us. The Church, founded by Jesus himself on the rock of Saint Peter (see Mt 16:18), has stood the test of time, trials, and countless tribulations. And the Church isn't just a cold institution imposing rules and regulations on her members. Everything she does and offers is with our best interests in mind. In the Gospel of John, Jesus says that he came to give us abundant life (10:10). So much of that abundance is there for us within the teachings and structure of the Catholic Church — but, especially as adults, it's up to us to take the time to explore and learn.

Sadly, many of us hardly know where to begin.

If you're anything like me and my husband before we began our journey back into the Catholic Church, chances are you haven't thought much about what "church" really means beyond the doors of your local parish. For many of us, when it comes to our personal, everyday lives, we figure "church" pretty much begins and ends there. If we want to be active and engaged, we can volunteer with parish ministries (which is a good and worthwhile thing to do). But do we really recognize just how much the Church should be part of our lives and decisions, no matter where we are, whether in the church hall or in our own living room? I know I didn't. That is, not until I came in contact with the treasure trove of Church teachings, which helped me see just how up close and personal our life of faith should be. It's all about a relationship.

Scripture

As we were returning to the Catholic Church, my husband and I became involved in a nondenominational Bible study. Back in the early 1990s, at least in our area, there weren't many Scripture-based studies for Catholics — at least none that we were aware of. We were still Christian newbies on so many levels, so when Dominick received a personal invitation to this Bible study, we decided that, at least for the time being, when it came to learning about the Bible, this was the best place for us.

We were surprised by a question often asked by the Protestants in the study with us: they wanted to know whether we had "a personal relationship" with Jesus. Had we accepted him as our "personal" Lord and Savior? That terminology wasn't commonly used by Catholics, and we weren't sure what it meant. Yet the more we studied the Bible together, the more this idea of a "personal" relationship with a very "personal" Savior began to make sense.

Through our Scripture study, we really got to know Jesus much more personally. He became real to us as we encountered him in the Gospels and began to learn just how much God loves us. We also realized what a treasure we have in the Catholic Church when it comes to developing that one-on-one relationship with God.

A few years after coming back to the Church, my husband and I heard a great homily on the importance of Scripture in our lives. The priest told the congregation to think of the word "Bible" as an acronym: *Basic Instructions Before Leaving Earth*. That has stuck with me ever since, and it encouraged us to continue to read the Bible daily.

If studying the Bible seems intimidating or overwhelming to you, no worries. If you don't have time to enroll in one of the many wonderful Catholic Bible studies, no worries there either. There are many great resources available online that can help you make Scripture a part of your everyday life, and it only takes a few minutes. Once you start reading Scripture, you won't be able to stop (and I'll bet you'll find yourself enrolled in one of those studies sooner than later). Today's Catholic Bible studies are well written and easy to follow, and most come with a video or online lecture plus questions for further reflection. One of the most encouraging aspects of joining a Bible study is being able to hear the insights of other participants. It's exciting to see and hear how God is working in someone else's life and how a particular Scripture passage made a difference for that person.

A great place to begin diving into Scripture, as we mentioned before, is with the daily readings for the Mass. Yep. Like so many other things, there is indeed an app for that. You'll find a number of links in our Beyond Sunday Resource List. Doing the daily Mass readings helps you not only learn and understand Scripture, but it also keeps you connected to the universal Catholic Church. Every Catholic in the world follows the same cycle of readings. You can even hear and read the pope's reflections on the readings by visiting a number of websites, which are provided for you, again, in our resource section.

Meeting God in His Church

Our Protestant friends were on to something when they talked about how we need to have a personal friendship with God. Yet the Catholic Church actually offers the most direct means for that encounter to take place in our lives. Having a personal relationship with God doesn't mean we can go it alone in a "Jesus and me" approach. Instead, we need the Church for that personal relationship. As Archbishop Vigneron points out in *Unleash the Gospel*:

> The Church is the context given by God in which we encounter Jesus Christ. Although it is common for people today to say they are "spiritual but not religious," or that they believe in Jesus but not the Church, in truth there can be no relationship with Jesus that does not include his Church. God relates to his people not as isolated individuals but as a people, a family, united with one another in deep bonds of love (Eph 4:1–6).[22]

Jesus invites us to have a personal relationship with him in the context of his Body, the Church. Our personal friendship with him starts in that context, in that community. We meet him in a very special way in the sacraments. The Eucharist, especially, is the place where we can foster the most personal relationship with God, because that's where we receive Christ — body, blood, soul, and divinity. That's where we become one with him.

In addition to reading Scripture, reading what the Church has to say about the sacraments, starting with the Eucharist, can really help you meet Jesus at an up-close and personal level. There are so many great writings on the Eucharist from our saints, popes, and other Church leaders, past and present. One of my favorite teachers on all things Catholic, including the gift of Eucharist, is Pope Saint John Paul II, one of the most beloved popes in modern times.

I know that reading Church documents might sound intimidating at first. We tend to think that such writings are only for priests or theologians. But if you look closely at the first few words of the documents written by the popes, you'll see that these documents are written for all of us in the Church. Saint John Paul II addressed his encyclical letter on the Eucharist (*Ecclesia de Eucharistia*) not only to bishops, priests, deacons, and consecrated people but also to "all the lay faithful" — that includes you and me!

As a bit of an introduction, or perhaps a refresher course, if you've read some Church documents but haven't visited them in a while, take a few minutes to slowly read the beautiful words from John Paul II on just how up close and personal Jesus is to us in the Sacrament of the Eucharist. I am sure you'll agree that you don't need to be a great theologian to grasp their meaning:

> The Church draws her life from the Eucharist. This truth does not simply express a daily experience of faith, but recapitulates *the heart of the mystery of the Church*. In a variety of ways she joyfully experiences the constant fulfillment of the promise: "Lo, I am with you always, to the close of the age" (Mt 28:20), but in the Holy Eucharist, through the changing of bread and wine into the body and blood of the Lord, she rejoices in this presence with unique intensity. Ever since Pentecost, when the Church, the People of the New Covenant, began her pilgrim journey towards her heavenly homeland, the Divine Sacrament has continued to mark the passing of her days, filling them with confident hope.
>
> The Second Vatican Council rightly proclaimed that the Eucharistic sacrifice is "the source and summit of the Christian life" (Dogmatic Constitution on the Church, *Lumen Gentium*,

11). "For the most holy Eucharist contains the Church's entire spiritual wealth: Christ himself, our passover and living bread. Through his own flesh, now made living and life-giving by the Holy Spirit, he offers life to men" (Decree on the Ministry and Life of Priests [*Presbyterorum Ordinis*], 5). Consequently the gaze of the Church is constantly turned to her Lord, present in the Sacrament of the Altar, in which she discovers the full manifestation of his boundless love.[23]

This is only one tiny example of the immense treasury of writings contained in the Church. I can't urge you strongly enough to begin reading what our popes and other leaders in the Church have written to help us grow in our faith. In my own case, after a while, Dominick and I just couldn't get enough of Jesus and our newly discovered faith. We wanted to help other Catholics access these documents, as we found them so enriching.

As we became more involved in our local Catholic parish, we began to volunteer with the marriage preparation program. Since much of our journey home was based on the healing of our relationship, we thought that volunteering with the marriage prep program would be a great way to thank God for what he had done in our lives. Little did we know we would gain so much more than we gave.

Part of the requirement to help the engaged couples prepare for marriage was to read some of the Church writings on the Sacrament of Matrimony. My husband and I had been married over ten years at that point, but we had no idea that the Church had so much to offer regarding married life. Surprised by this discovery, we began to crack open other Church teachings as well. It was like an entirely new world opened to us, as we slowly became exposed to the incredible amount of resources, documents, Church councils, writings, events, and celebrations, not to mention the witness of thousands of saints, that beautifully, intimately, and *personally* pertain to our daily concerns and interests.

Over time, we also discovered a long line of kindred spirits in the saints. Thanks to years in Catholic school, I knew many of them by name, but now they were no longer just stories in a book or images and statues on a shelf. I could relate to them because I learned they each had their own set of issues and problems to overcome. They were real people who made a real difference while fighting persistently against their real weaknesses and challenges. They were brothers and sisters to whom I could relate in so many ways.

Even though I had been raised Catholic and thought I had a general grasp of what the Faith taught and why, I quickly learned the extent of what I didn't know and what I was missing. My husband experienced something very similar. It was amazing. It was also, in many ways, a real wake-up call. We felt as though we were appearing in our own Catholic version of an old beverage commercial: "Wow. Where have I been all these years? I could have had a V8!"

Over the years, my husband and I continue to have all sorts of these "V8 moments." We are consistently amazed to discover that the Church offers us so much that allows us to live a full, abundant life. And trust me on this: once you start to know the Church in a more up-close and personal way, you will soon become the "V8 type" yourself.

The Church has this amazing treasure trove of teachings tailor-made to fit real people — people like you and me — in our day-to-day lives. And for too many years, I had no idea any of this existed. To top it off, I was an award-winning journalist, who got assigned to cover Church events! I was supposed to be informed and "in the know." Yet, if I didn't know about these things, how many practicing Catholics whose day job doesn't have those requirements, who attend Mass week after week, have no idea what the Church has to offer?

So where does this leave you when it comes to going beyond Sunday? How do you begin to tap into these resources if you've never read a letter from your own bishop, let alone the pope? Well, for starters, begin with your particular areas of interests and your personal challenges. Simply going to the home page of the United States Conference of Catholic Bishops (www.usccb.org), for example, will lead you to countless documents, not to mention interesting articles, prayer campaigns, and instructional videos, as well as statements on all kinds of efforts underway by the Church as part of the continual outreach to those in need. The USCCB also has a super-convenient link to the daily Mass readings.

Your own parish bulletin has a lot more to offer than just the latest birth announcements, baptisms, and bingo gatherings. Most of these bulletins, as well as parish websites, can be a wealth of resources for what's happening at your own parish and in your diocese. Speaking of which, when was the last time you visited your diocesan website to see what your bishop has to say?

Our bishops and Church leaders are not hiding out in monasteries somewhere in the mountains. Oh, sure, there are religious orders whose vocation is centered around a cloistered prayer life. But our leaders, especially after learning much from the Church's problems that have become very public, are sincerely trying to "smell like the sheep," as Pope Francis has urged them. Our bishops want to relate to Catholics and help them apply their faith to their everyday lives, and to look at everything, as my friend and Catholic radio colleague, Al Kresta, always says, "through the lenses of Scripture and the teachings of the Church." They share with us solid insights on issues affecting our culture.

As an example, one major issue that has come to light recently is the huge problem of sexual harassment in our culture. Ever since the Hollywood sex scandal that began with the Harvey Weinstein allegations in the fall of 2017, several movements have been formed to raise awareness and find solutions. I don't know anyone who disagrees that this is not just a problem; it's an epidemic to which no organization, workplace, or entity is immune. It happens in all areas of society, in some much more frequently than others. But it's not a stretch to say it's just about everywhere. Ever wonder what the Church has to say about this topic and about the roles of women and men in society and how they relate to one another in general? You might be surprised.

Archbishop Samuel J. Aquila of Denver, Colorado, addressed the sexual harassment issue in his monthly column, released in December 2017, as the stories were still breaking:

> History teaches that sexual harassment is hardly new, but the extent and bald belligerence of it are new. Predatory sexual behavior runs the gamut from politicians and Hollywood luminaries, to journalists, artists, and — as the Church has learned the hard way — even clergy. There are many factors that have contributed to this epidemic in our culture.

The archbishop then went on to help Catholics draw from Church teaching on the topic. This issue is deeply rooted in our understanding of the dignity of each human being made in the image and likeness of God. I think he really hit the nail on the head, referring to *Humanae Vitae*, an important and not always popular document on human sexuality released by Pope Saint Paul VI in the tumultuous 1960s:

Even though he was being pressured to change the Church's teaching on contraception, Blessed Paul VI prayerfully and wisely taught that the unitive and procreative aspects of sex cannot be separated without causing significant damage. He predicted that doing so would lower morality, increase marital infidelity, cause men to lose respect for women, and allow governments to use contraceptives in a coercive manner.

Blessed Paul VI's prophetic insights have unhappily come to pass with the widespread use of contraception. His prediction about a loss of respect for women is quite relevant to the discussion about sexual harassment. He wrote: "a man who grows accustomed to the use of contraceptive methods may forget the reverence due to a woman, and, disregarding her physical and emotional equilibrium, reduce her to being a mere instrument for the satisfaction of his own desires ..." (HV, 17).

It is too simplistic to say that the increase in sexual harassment can entirely be linked to the widespread usage of contraception, but the role it has played in turning sex into a commodity and in objectifying women is undeniable.[24]

Saint John Paul II once said that truth never changes. We can learn more about a particular truth over time, but truth itself does not change. Again, as Archbishop Aquila pointed out, what about the truth concerning the dignity of the human person? This is where the culture has gotten it all wrong. When we fail to see every person as a dignified brother or sister made in the image and likeness of God, and instead view or treat them as objects, we all suffer the consequences, which is exactly what we're seeing playing out in the world currently.

Many other Church documents deal with this exact issue, as well as others connected to it, such as feminism. These documents include, but are certainly not limited to, the following, by Saint John Paul II:

- *Mulieris Dignitatem* (On the Dignity and Vocation of Women), 1998
- Letter to Women (1995)
- *Evangelium Vitae* (*The Gospel of Life*), 1995

Another example of the Church offering advice for our daily lives is the yearly papal statements issued on World Communications Day. What parent isn't concerned about media influence on their children? Yet, how many Catholic moms and dads, or Catholics in general for that matter, are aware of these annual statements? They are short, to the point, and extremely helpful when it comes to how Catholics can use the media wisely. They contain practical advice on media usage for everyone, especially the family. One of my favorite statements, from John Paul II in 2004, is entitled "The Media and the Family: A Risk and a Richness,"[25] in which he highlighted the pros and cons of media outlets in the family and how Catholics are to be engaged in media awareness and activism.

These are just a few examples of what the Church has to offer. It doesn't matter what topic or issue you start with — just get started. If you have questions, you'll see that the Church has the answers that will help us in our efforts to have a truly up-close and personal relationship with God.

MONDAY

Reflect: Do you see God more as a judgmental rule-maker or as a loving and merciful Father? What influences the way you view God?

TUESDAY

Reflect: Spend a few minutes today pondering Jesus' words in John 10:10: "I came that they may have life, and have it abundantly." Where do you think Jesus might be inviting you to live a more abundant life?

WEDNESDAY

Pray: Ask God to help you to see what roadblocks are keeping you from living that abundant life.

THURSDAY

Act: Subscribe to an online inspirational daily email, such as those listed in the Beyond Sunday Resource List.

FRIDAY

Act: Investigate what opportunities are being offered in your parish or in a nearby parish or other online studies listed in the resource section of this book that can help you learn God's word and grow in your relationship with him and in your Catholic faith.

SATURDAY

Read & Reflect: Read and reflect on the readings for this Sunday: www.usccb.org/bible/readings.

CHAPTER SIX

The Three M's of Faith

Meeting, Mercy, and Mission

"Come, see a man who told me all that I ever did."
— JOHN 4:29

In February 2016, I was speaking at a women's conference in Minneapolis. The theme of the event was built around the Year of Mercy, a special year in the Church set aside by Pope Francis to encourage Catholics, especially those who have fallen away, to come home and freely receive the mercy of God. By a beautiful coincidence (of course, there's no such thing), the scheduled Gospel for the Mass that weekend spoke directly to the theme of the women's conference — a theme that now touches deeply on our journey beyond Sunday.

The Gospel was John 4:1–42, which details the exchange between Jesus and the Samaritan woman at the well. Perhaps you have heard this story many times before, or maybe you're not very familiar with it. Either way, I encourage you to set this book down, right now, open your Bible, and read this passage.

The celebrant, recognizing the connection between the day's Gospel and our conference, took us deeply into the reading to show us how it applies to our lives today. As I was listening to him that cold Saturday afternoon, his words about Jesus warmed my heart and made so much sense. He talked about the three-pronged approach all of us need to take when it comes to our relationship with God. I like to refer to this approach as the "three *M*'s of faith": Meeting, Mercy, and Mission.

When we encounter or meet God, if we are truly open as the Samaritan woman was, Jesus shows us how much he loves us by showing us mercy. It's not about condemnation. It's about love and reconciliation. Once we receive that love and mercy, we are grateful for the opportunity to begin again, and we set out on a new mission of faith.

Meeting

The Samaritan woman was an outcast because she was living with a man who was not her husband. She also had had five husbands in her past. In order to avoid the snubs and glares from the townspeople, she would go to the well to fetch water at about noon. In that part of the world, noon is the hottest part of the day, and most people do not go outside at that time, if they can avoid it. This meant that she would, for the most part, be alone. She could get her water and head back home, hopefully without being noticed. Except this time, when she arrived at the well, someone was waiting for her. And that someone just happened to be God himself.

Her meeting, or initial encounter, with Christ, was the beginning of a new life for this woman. Jesus told her about her own life and how she was selling herself short. He didn't condemn her. Instead, he showed her how her daily trips to the well weren't ever going to satisfy her. She would be forever going back to that same well without her thirst being quenched. "Every one who drinks of this water will thirst again," he told her.

Yet he doesn't leave it there — he has something better to offer: "but whoever drinks of the water that I shall give him will never thirst; the water that I shall give him will become in him a spring of water welling up to eternal life" (Jn 4:13–15).

Isn't that sense of being constantly thirsty for something, even if we don't know what it is, a feeling we all know too well? How many times have we accomplished a goal or obtained something that we thought would definitely make a major difference in our level of happiness, only to feel empty or parched a short time later? Then we start searching for something else, and the cycle begins all over again.

I can relate, believe me. For years, I bought into the lie that the way to true happiness was self-fulfillment. For me and a lot of another people, that translated into sacrificing everything for a successful career. But no matter how many exclusive news reports I filed or how many journalism awards I won, there was always something missing. I kept going back to the well time and time again, only to come up empty.

I settled for the way of the world, just as the Samaritan woman has settled for that. For her, having a man in her life and a decently comfortable home were everything. Yet her search for these things left her empty, as she cycled through five marriages. And when she met Jesus, she was living with a man who was not her husband. Maybe she figured this was the best she could do. Hey, at least she had a roof over her head and companionship. Could it be that, for her, the shame and the embarrassment were heavy loads but not heavier than the fear of loneliness?

For me, at least I had a good job and was making a name for myself. The heavy burdens of long nights, missed holidays, and one too many weekend shifts were a trade-off for the brass ring. Newswomen just didn't put family first. Women in my business who dared to pay attention to anything other than their careers were looked down upon as weak and overly emotional. So, I put on a brave face and repeatedly tried to ignore the fact that making a name for myself in the competitive world of broadcast news was making me absolutely miserable.

Where are you going in terms of your "meeting"? What brings you back to the well day after day? Is it someone you're hoping to encounter, or something such as the ultimate job, the new home, or the financial goals you've set for yourself? Where has that search left you in terms of true joy? And most importantly, where is that meeting with God in terms of your bucket list?

It's not that we shouldn't have career goals or want to make a good living to support ourselves and our families, but sometimes if we put too much emphasis on those things, as I did, we find ourselves in a situation similar to the woman at the well, thirsting for more.

Mercy

Like the Samaritan woman, we might hide from God or others for fear of condemnation and rejection. It could be that, like me, your search has led you to a place of which you're not exactly proud. You have known that you needed to pay more attention to God, and possibly others in your life. But gradually you found yourself slipping away, and soon priorities were misplaced. Being ashamed can be the start of self-awareness — an awareness that recognizes an imbalance in our life that needs correcting. God doesn't want us to hide from him and stay stuck in our shame. When Christ meets us, he shows us — as he showed the woman at the well — nothing but mercy.

Let's think about this for a minute, looking at the Gospel story. There was the initial encounter with Christ at the well. He entered into a real conversation with the woman. His gentle approach enabled her to open up and admit the truth to Jesus. He, unlike other people in her town and in her life, did not condemn her, in spite of everything she had done. Because of his genuine interest and concern, she was able to move past her shame and receive his gift of mercy. She felt like a new person, inside and out, because she met the Messiah, and the Messiah cared deeply about her. She was so moved by the experience that, as Saint John's Gospel tells us, she forgot all about the task at hand that day (fetching water). Now, all of a sudden, she had much more important work to do.

While I never had five husbands, and am blessed to be married to the same wonderful man for over thirty years now, I, too, was ashamed of the way I had ignored my relationship and was living. Once I was able to crack open the door to my heart, even a little bit, to allow Jesus in, he showed me that I deserved better than to be a slave to the world's condition of happiness. My husband, my marriage, and, most importantly, my relationship with God were timeless treasures that I needed to cherish and nurture. Like the Samaritan woman, I didn't feel worthy, either. But after humbling myself and going to receive the Sacrament of Penance and Reconciliation, Jesus showed up, big time, and gave me abundant mercy and a brand-new mission.

Mercy is never far away. It's right down the block or around the corner at your local parish, and it starts with confession, as explained in the *Catechism*:

> "Those who approach the sacrament of Penance obtain pardon from God's mercy for the offense committed against him, and are, at the same time, reconciled with the Church which they have wounded by their sins and which by charity, by example, and by prayer labors for their conversion" (*Lumen Gentium*, 11.2).

It is called the *sacrament of conversion* because it makes sacramentally present Jesus' call to conversion, the first step in returning to the Father (cf. Mk 1:15; Lk 15:18) from whom one has strayed by sin. (CCC 1422–1423, emphasis in original)

We're not designed to keep everything, especially our troubles or mistakes, bottled up inside. Why is it that so many reality shows are focused on "true confessions," so to speak? Why do some feel the need to talk to a Jerry Springer or a Dr. Phil? Wouldn't you much rather talk to someone who is serving in the person of Christ or, as the Church says, "*in persona Christi*" than someone serving the ratings of a money-hungry TV network? Don't be afraid to open your heart to the Lord and to receive his mercy. He is waiting to give it.

Mission

The meeting with Christ and encounter with his mercy did not end there for the Samaritan woman. Instead, Saint John tells us:

So the woman left her water jar, and went away into the city, and said to the people, "Come see a man who told me all that I ever did. Can this be the Christ?" They went out of the city and were coming to him. (Jn 4:28–30)

Think about that for a minute. This woman, who had established a pattern of completing her chores without being seen or heard, suddenly became an evangelist. She ran to meet the people she'd been avoiding for so long, to speak to them face-to-face. She had a new mission. The result?

Many Samaritans from that city believed in him because of the woman's testimony. "He told me all that I ever did." So when the Samaritans came to him, they asked him to stay with them; and he stayed there two days. (Jn: 4:39–40)

And this is exactly what confession prepares us for, as the *Catechism* also explains:

It is called the *sacrament of Reconciliation*, because it imparts to the sinner the life of God who reconciles: "Be reconciled to God" (2 Cor 5:20). He who lives by God's merciful love is ready to respond to the Lord's call: "Go; first be reconciled to your brother" (Mt 5:24). (CCC 1424, emphasis in original).

....

It sounds scary doesn't it? When we hear or read about a mission, we might automatically think about missionaries in faraway places, such as the incredible missionary work of Saint Teresa of Calcutta. Okay, so the Mother Teresas of the world are few and far between. But here is the good news: we're not all called to be, nor are we all capable of being, a Mother Teresa — and even Mother Teresa said pretty much the same thing. She said, among other things, "If you can't feed a hundred people, then just feed one."

While Mother Teresa lived a simple and austere life, disconnected from the noise of the world, she certainly knew how to tap into those spiritual connections. These are the tools available to all of us that will help us discover our mission and lead us to exactly where we need to be.

When I returned to the secular media after my firing, things went fine, for a while. But I couldn't ignore that inner voice that kept telling me on some level that the news business just didn't feel right for me any longer. Suddenly, it was as though I was a foreigner in some strange land. Everyone was speaking a different language. I began to notice the many problems with my industry that I hadn't noticed before, including the emphasis on ratings, the "if it bleeds it leads" mentality, which resulted in me turning into what seemed like an ambulance chaser instead of a reporter, forever covering one car crash or house fire after another. And there was the media bias when it came to covering issues such as abortion and prayer in schools. I was becoming very disillusioned, even though, at that point, I wasn't ready to walk away just yet. It was something I began to think and pray about daily.

That voice inside me was the Holy Spirit, though I didn't fully recognize that at the time. I experienced it more as an instinct. At the time, I really didn't even know what I was doing when it came to incorporating spiritual practices into my life. I just knew that I needed to somehow figure out if a newsroom was where God still wanted me. I went about the business of working on my marriage and regularly seeking God in my life through Bible study, while all the time working as a TV news reporter and taking a closer look at the negative changes occurring in broadcast news and the media in general.

I think of the Holy Spirit's guidance as a Catholic GPS system that lets us know when we might be a little bit lost and need to start heading in a different direction. The Scripture along with Church teaching encourage us to listen to the Holy Spirit and to tap into the gifts and fruits of the Spirit. (You'll find more details on both in the resource section of this book.) As I went along trying to figure out what the heck my real calling was and where God wanted me to be, I tried to keep a positive attitude and be kind to those at work, even though at times I felt like punching them in the nose, given how rotten the business was getting. And I refused to let them steal my joy. Looking back, I think that was the fruits of the Holy Spirit in action in my life.

Eventually, I left the secular media, started my own speaking and communications ministry, and worked as a Catholic talk show host. Those developments and changes in my life were just that: developments that happened over a period of not just months of discernment and prayer but years.

That's how it is for most of us as we learn to follow where God is leading us. If we take our time, tapping into the gifts and fruits of the Spirit, the road map of our mission, our lives will slowly change and develop according to God's plan for us. Getting back to Saint Teresa of Calcutta, she was already serving as a religious sister when she heard her "call within a call": God telling her to go and serve a different group of people, the poorest of the poor in India and all over the world. Saint Teresa was always open to God's will. If we are open in the same way, we will find our calling, as well as possible additional calls.

In other words, your "mission" right now could be as simple as re-ordering some priorities and being the very best spouse and parent you can be. It could mean starting a Bible study at your parish or using your skills to help a particular ministry or charity.

And while it certainly would be a lot easier if God would just drop a big arrow from the sky pointing us directly to our mission, that's not the way it works. God is a gentleman, and among his greatest gifts is the gift of free will. He doesn't force himself on us. Even though his plan is always the best plan, because as our Creator he created us for a specific purpose and mission, we have to have the buy-in, so to speak, on our end. It's up to us to have an open heart exercising our free will with a "Yes, Lord."

Often when we take the first steps, we don't even know exactly what our mission is or where we're going. I didn't. I just knew that I no longer felt comfortable working in the news business. I didn't feel I was making a difference any longer, and I had a desire to use my talents more effectively and, most importantly, to share what I was learning about my Catholic faith and my knowledge about the media and its impact on all of us. So I took one step at a time, the first step being a pretty simple prayer:

> Okay Lord. Whatever you want me to do with my gift of gab, show me. However you want to use my communications talents, point me in the right direction.

I kept praying that prayer daily. And little by little, step by step, God led me from one point to the next. I never knew when I walked away from the news business nearly twenty years ago that I would eventually become a Catholic journalist and talk show host. But looking back, it all makes sense now. Everything I did back then, honing my skills as an interviewer, an investigator, and a reporter, broadcasting live several times a day in some pretty tough conditions, was excellent training for my current mission. I use the word "current" because I still say the same prayer today that I said when I left the news media. It's my reminder to be open to whatever God has in store.

. . . .

Responding to the Lord's call starts with a meeting. In that meeting, if we are willing to take that first step, God gives us mercy. When we receive his mercy, everything changes. We're so grateful that we just can't keep it to ourselves, and we begin a brand-new mission. Maybe your ministry won't be a public mission or evangelization. Every person's mission is unique. But wherever God calls you, you can count on this: things will change for the better. God keeps his promises.

Being open to God's call or "mission" for you is key for two main reasons. First, it is the only thing that is going to make you truly joyful. And second, your mission, or calling, is bigger than you, because how each of us lives our life greatly affects others. Consider what one of my favorite saints, Catherine of Siena, had to say about our mission or calling: "When we are who we are called to be, we will set the world ablaze."

Amen!

Going
BEYOND *Sunday*

MONDAY

Reflect: Where is the "well" in your life? Does it fill you up or leave you empty?

TUESDAY

Read: Reread John 4:1–42 about the Samaritan woman.

WEDNESDAY

Act: Jesus has a unique mission for each one of us. What do you think he's calling you to do? Where might he be asking you to share his mercy and love with others?

THURSDAY

Reflect: Reflect upon the Beatitudes (listed in Beyond Sunday Resource List of this book). Consider which one God might be calling you to focus on living out better right now.

FRIDAY

Act: Everyone has unique gifts and talents to share. Look in your parish bulletin at the list of ministries and activities going on for opportunities and consider sharing your God-given talents.

SATURDAY

Read & Reflect: Read and reflect on the readings for this Sunday: www.usccb.org/bible/readings.

CHAPTER SEVEN

Five Cures for the Common Catholic Cold

....

"Evangelizing aims to lead others to life-changing encounters with Jesus, with the result that he becomes the Lord of one's life."[26]
— ARCHBISHOP ALLEN H. VIGNERON

We all know how nagging the common cold can be. It sneaks up on us before we even realize it. We might think we're doing a good job of protecting ourselves and keeping ourselves strong and healthy. But despite our efforts, we can easily be infected.

The common Catholic cold is a lot like a bad bug that's going around. Just like the physical version has its symptoms, so does this spiritual version. It's a culmination of some of our common Catholic ailments highlighted earlier. When we catch a cold, we can suffer from one, several, or even all of the uncomfortable related conditions. It would be great to think that the common Catholic cold is a once-in-a-lifetime illness. But, here again, just as adults can easily catch the common cold as often as twice a year, the same thing can happen to us on a faith or spiritual level if we take our relationship with God for granted.

Unfortunately, once the common Catholic cold starts to spread, it can have a major ripple effect, not all that different from the coughing, sneezing type of illness. It definitely affects us, quickly slowing us down and making us feel tired, achy, run-down, and lethargic. So, what are the best remedies for avoiding the common Catholic cold? How can we keep ourselves spiritually healthy and ward off worse conditions like Catholic Curmudgeonitis or Christeritis?

Consider the following action items as your spiritual vitamin C: your heavenly glass of OJ or the bowl of chicken soup for the soul that certainly can't hurt, and in the long run will help keep you strong. Of course, we'll never be free of all our issues, whether physical or spiritual, until we get to heaven. And given that we're human, we're bound to catch another cold now and then, but the more we get fit faithwise, the better off we'll be.

1. If God Is Your Co-pilot, Change Seats

You've probably seen those clever bumper stickers, the ones with cute sayings that make us smile or think happy thoughts while we're stuck in heavy traffic on the way to the office or the supermarket. Some of the more popular ones sport messages of a spiritual nature. There's a particular saying that caught my attention a few years after I came back to the Church. It caught my attention because it described in a few short words how I once lived my life. In my case, it prompted challenging rather than happy thoughts, as it reminded me of how I was always trying, despite my repeated lack of success, to be in control.

The bumper sticker read: "God is my co-pilot."

At first glance, this saying seems very thoughtful. The person behind the wheel of the vehicle advertising this message must certainly be driving down the right road. After all, they obviously consult God on at least a semi-regular basis if they have him as their co-pilot. Shouldn't that be the goal for all of us?

Actually, not quite. As we grow in our appreciation and understanding of who God is, it becomes apparent that this slogan actually encapsulates a big problem in our society today: our need to continually call the shots according to our own agenda. Especially in our comfortable Western world, we like to keep God close enough to consult or call on him when we hit a few bumps in the road. We're okay with him hanging out in the passenger seat, but heaven forbid we allow him to take the wheel. Just think about it for a minute. How arrogant are we to claim that the Alpha and the Omega, the Beginning and the End, the Creator of the universe, is our co-pilot? This kind of thinking leads us to view ourselves as equal to — or, in an even worse-case scenario, more important than — our Maker.

So, step number one, if we really want to go beyond Sunday: If God is your co-pilot, then, for crying out loud, change seats!

If we need a few reminders about how God is God and we are not, all we need to do is refer to the Bible. As I mentioned earlier, I often tell folks to think of the word "Bible" as an acronym: Basic Instructions Before Leaving Earth. The Bible is full of beautiful verses on the power of God. These verses can help calm us down when we feel like we've got to be in complete control. Just a quick glance at Scripture can have a sobering and shrinking effect on our egos — and that's a good thing.

In Romans 11:33 we read: "O the depth of the riches and wisdom and knowledge of God! How unsearchable are his judgments and how inscrutable his ways!"

In the Old Testament, God speaks to the prophet Jeremiah, bringing us a crucial question we have to ponder if we claim to believe in God: "Can a man hide himself in secret places so that I cannot see him? says the LORD. Do I not fill heaven and earth? says the LORD" (Jer 23:24).

Or, if we're still not convinced of who is really in charge and driving this bus called life, let's go back all the way to the beginning with the Book of Genesis, specifically Genesis 1:1: "In the beginning God created the heavens and the earth."

The bottom line is that if we want to see God work in our lives, and if we truly want to grow in our relationship with him, we have to submit to his will and believe in our hearts that he is our loving Father. And Father really does know best. He wants us to be truly happy, but he is a gentleman and will not force his will on us. If we are willing to put God first and say, "Jesus, I trust in you," then he will be able to work in our lives. It starts first with our complete "yes" — and getting out of the driver's seat.

2. Read God's Love Letter

The second step to prevent the common Catholic cold: Read God's love letter to us — the Bible. As mentioned earlier in the "Up Close and Personal" chapter, talk about curing what ails you. God's love letter will make you feel like you could not only run but win the Boston Marathon. It's that powerful.

When we fall in love with someone, we want to know what they're thinking, their likes and dislikes, and how they feel about particular issues. We do our best to get to know their family and friends, because it helps us get to know the love of our life even better. We also do our best to communicate with them. Whether it's in person, on the phone, Skype, another text message, or email, we keep in regular contact. Often, we keep the messages they send us as mementos.

Well, if you love God, one of the best ways to get to know him intimately is by reading his love letter, the Bible. In the Bible, we learn about God's family, what breaks his heart, what makes him happy, and how we can stay in relationship with him. All of this and more just by picking up the Bible for a few minutes every day.

Imagine if you showed up at the dinner table every day and merely exchanged formalities with your spouse or other family members. Imagine if you never consulted them on important matters in your life and treated them as mere acquaintances or roommates, not really needing, wanting, or valuing their input at all. Hard to picture, isn't it? Yet this is what we're saying to God when we don't even try to listen to what he tells us in Scripture.

The Catholic Church gives us a lot of help when it comes to studying the Bible. We don't even have to worry about where to begin! First of all, the Church lays out daily readings, which are read and prayed by Catholics throughout the world in the Church's daily liturgy, as well as the Mass each Sunday.

Mass is celebrated daily around the world. During the weekday Masses (unlike Sunday), there are only three readings: the first reading (from either the Old or New Testament), the responsorial psalm, and the Gospel. These readings are easily found online, and there are plenty of hard-copy devotionals available with solid reflections to help you get the most out of the Scriptures. These reflections are helpful if you, like me, often find yourself scratching your head trying to figure out what message God is trying to get across to you today. You can even have the daily readings sent directly to your email inbox from the United States Conference of Catholic Bishops (www.usccb.org/bible/readings/111517 .cfm).

If you want to dive deeper, there are also a number of wonderful Scripture studies you can do, whether on your own, as a couple, or even in a group at the home or parish level (more information can be found in the Beyond Sunday Resource List).

If we put forth the effort, little by little, day by day, we will get to know God as we encounter him in his word and allow it to take root and grow in our hearts and souls.

3. Consider the Source

If we really want our faith to go beyond Sunday, we've got to be careful about what things we allow to influence our lives, our thinking, and our actions. These things can creep in without us even being aware of them, laying us low with the common Catholic cold before we know it, which makes them all the more dangerous. So, before we can go any further, we need to do a little soul-searching. It's time to reflect: what sources have you allowed to influence and form your thoughts and opinions? The answers might surprise you.

It helps to ask yourself a few key questions:

- Do I struggle with any particular Church teachings? If so, which ones and why?
- Where have I gotten my information about various teachings of the Church, especially the ones I find challenging? Have I consulted any Church documents about these teachings?
- In my struggles or possible disagreements with the Church, have I attempted to talk to a priest or someone else knowledgeable in Church teaching?
- How often, if ever, have I consulted the *Catechism of the Catholic Church* regarding matters of faith and morals?
- How many solid Catholic media outlets (as opposed to CNN, Fox News, MSNBC, etc.) have I turned to in trying to gain a deeper understanding of my Catholic faith?

These are just a few of the questions my husband and I struggled with on our way back to the Church. We realized that, for the most part, our catechesis ended when we received the Sacrament of Confirmation. After that, we allowed ourselves to be formed by the messages of the culture. We soon realized, as we began to read Scripture and take our faith seriously, that we had been sorely misled by secular sources that misunderstood and misrepresented Church teaching.

When we began to dive into the beautiful writings of the saints and recent popes, we fell head over heels in love with Jesus and Catholicism. A whole new world opened up to us. So, I speak from experience when I say, do yourself a favor: start spending less time with secular sources and more time with Catholic outlets. Consult the Beyond Sunday Resource List for some great ideas on how to find out what the Church really teaches, especially in those areas where you may find yourself wrestling with the Faith. You might be surprised to find out just how much these teachings are focused on your ultimate good — not to squash your fun or make you miserable. In fact, just the opposite. And again, I speak from experience: living by these teachings will make you happier than you've ever been.

4. Don't Just Do Something, Sit There

Sometimes we need not just to slow down but also to take some time to do nothing. Believe it or not, this is an important part of going beyond Sunday and staying spiritually healthy.

My Italian ancestors call this *dolce far niente*: the art or sweetness of doing nothing. It might sound crazy, but it's rooted in Scripture. In Psalm 46:10 the Lord reminds us, "Be still, and know that I am God." And doing nothing, although it is so contrary to our busy-bee American way of life, is essential when it comes to allowing ourselves to slow down and be with no one else but God.

In today's crazy, "microwave" society, where everything seems to happen at breakneck speed, few of us slow down to do much of anything. We eat on the go, text behind the wheel, talk on the phone while doing a number of other tasks, and by the time we get home at night, we hit the pillow completely exhausted — only to start the same insane schedule over again the next morning. I once heard it said that Christians should think of the word "busy" as another important acronym: "**B**eing **U**nder **S**atan's **Y**oke." While of course there will always be tasks to complete at work, laundry to do at home, and a long list of other must-do projects, we've taken busy to an extreme where it is pulling us in all kinds of directions and, namely, away from God.

We have little time to really think, reflect, and ponder what God might be trying to show us, teach us, or tell us. Most importantly, we don't give ourselves time just to be with him and keep him company. Obviously, that makes it really hard to have a real relationship with him. And that's not to mention the impact it has on our other relationships — with our spouse, in our family, and in our broader communities.

Here's a sobering statistic: research shows that married couples only spend about thirty minutes of alone time together per week. They may be in the house together, but they're usually surrounded by children and a swirl of many other activities. If we're only giving our spouses thirty minutes of up-close and personal time per week, how much is left for God?

You might say, well I spend at least an hour a week with God at Mass. Okay, but think back to the last Sunday Mass you attended. Do you really remember the homily or the Gospel message? Were you completely attentive to God the whole time, or did your mind wander? Were you worried about problems at work or at home that distracted some of your attention? Did you look at your watch, wondering when Mass would end, so that you could get on with your very busy schedule? I'm not saying this to make you feel bad. It happens to all of us. Anyone who says they never get distracted during Mass is either a saint or not being honest with themselves or others. The point I'm trying to make is that we're never going to be able to get beyond Sunday if we don't spend more time with Jesus. And one, often distracted, hour at Mass each week probably isn't enough to keep our relationship with him strong and healthy.

In order to grow, we need to recharge and refocus, and one of the best ways to do that is to spend time just sitting and doing nothing with God. How this happens is entirely up to you. One suggestion would be to find a parish near you that has Eucharistic Adoration. Sitting before Jesus in the monstrance is a deeply moving way to just be in his presence. You don't have to even say anything. Just be still and let him do the talking.

Slowing down eases our stress levels and helps us get reconnected with God and with our families. It has a positive ripple effect that can be felt throughout our life. As that old cereal commercial used to claim: "Try it, you'll like it." Doing nothing, or being still, is really the art of doing the most important thing of all.

5. Silence the Noise

During an address he gave while visiting his native Germany in 2006, Pope Benedict XVI raised concerns about the impact of noise, noise, and more noise on Christians and their relationship with God: "Put simply, we are no longer able to hear God — there are too many different frequencies filling our ears."[27]

Fast forward to spring 2016, and Benedict XVI would find a friend in country singer Kenny Chesney, who released a hit single, "Noise." In the song, Chesney laments, "Seems like all we ever hear is noise."

Believe it or not, we live in such a noisy, stress-filled, hectic world that even a country music superstar is commenting on it. In an interview for the release of the single in spring 2016, Chesney told reporters he was hoping to get his fans to do more than just snap their fingers and tap their toes. He wanted them to really think about all the noise in our lives: "We have all these devices that have changed our way of thinking. Now we're lost in this cloud of trying to communicate and multitasking."

To make matters worse, Chesney believes we've become so accustomed to all the noise that we are drawn to it: "I think a lot of what is drowning things out is just sensational stuff to get us hooked. It seems like we're all drawn to chaos or a carnival that's noise in itself."

Unfortunately, too few of us even make an attempt to take control of the media that make our world so very noisy. According to the latest research, young people — namely, those at the grade school and high school level — consume around fifty-three hours of media per week. Adults aren't doing much better, spending about as much time with tech toys as on the job — about forty to forty-five hours of media time per week.

Being a Catholic radio and television host, I would like to think that all of those folks consuming double-digit amounts of media are glued to EWTN or other Catholic outlets, but that's simply not the reality. Most of the media time is spent consuming messages contrary to Christian (especially Catholic Christian) beliefs. Even if we are tuning into Catholic or other wholesome media outlets, silencing the noise is still something that is good for the body and the soul.

It's probably not much of a stretch to say that spending umpteen hours in front of the TV screen with all those commercials, not to mention ridiculous reality shows featuring lifestyles of the rich, famous, and frivolous, doesn't do much to help bring us peace. And what about the violence and the sexual content? Those images and messages must do a number on our psyche and our spirit.

According to some studies, tuning out can actually reduce stress in our lives. This is especially true when it comes to social media. A few years ago, some writers at the *Huffington Post* decided to see the connection between our high usage of social media and levels of stress. They did some digging through the many studies out there and found, in fact, there was a strong connection. Social media users were at least

14 percent more likely than nonusers to characterize their lives as "somewhat stressful":

> Like it or not, social media is one of the most prevalent ways people learn about new movies, music, fashion, books, or other products. Twenty-eight percent of people say their friends on social media influence the music they listen to, 36 percent the TV shows and movies they watch, and 36 percent the brands and products they buy.
>
> All of this influence appears to correlate closely with stress. People who say social media influences the products they buy "a lot" are 45 percent more likely to say their lives are "very stressful." Maybe we can't afford all the fancy new products our friends are buying. Maybe we're too busy to follow the trends in music or fashion. Whatever the reason, it's evident that the more we pay attention to our friends' activities, tastes, and possessions, the more stress we report in our lives.[28]

Trying to reduce the noise in our lives doesn't mean that we have to live the life of a hermit in total solitude or silence. After all, the Church teaches us that the media, and nowadays social media especially, have proven to be an effective tool for evangelization. Social media is also a convenient and affordable way to stay connected with family and friends. In the end, it's really all about balance and knowing when to put down the phone, back away from the computer, turn off that TV, and spend time first and foremost with God.

To keep on going beyond Sunday, we need to take silence back. Make time for silence every day if you can, even if it's just in the car on your way home from work. Turn off the noise, tune out, and you'll be amazed at the change.

Going BEYOND Sunday

MONDAY

Reflect: How can you put God in the driver's seat today?

TUESDAY

Reflect: How can you boost your spiritual immune system to fight back against the common Catholic cold in the future?

WEDNESDAY

Act: Look at your media usage and where you are getting your news and information. Find out if there's a Catholic radio station, TV, or newspaper in your local area. Listen online through your Bluetooth; check out the many great Catholic podcasts (many of which are listed in the resource section of this book).

THURSDAY

Act: Search in your phone's app store for the word "Catholic." Download a Catholic app to help you spend more time with God each day. Put a reminder on your phone daily to check out the app, or at least to stop and pray and listen to God.

FRIDAY

Pray: Spend ten minutes today in silence listening to God. What is he saying to you?

SATURDAY

Read & Reflect: Read and reflect on the readings for this Sunday: www.usccb.org/bible/readings.

CHAPTER EIGHT

"God Gives Us What We Need Wrapped in What We Want"

....

> *"For I know the plans I have for you, says the LORD, plans for welfare*
> *and not for evil, to give you a future and a hope."*
> — JEREMIAH 29:11

Look at that chapter title again: *"God gives us what we need wrapped in what we want."*

This profound statement is the brainchild of Jeff Cavins, well-known Scripture scholar, author, speaker, and Bible-study leader, who is also regularly featured on Catholic radio and TV. Jeff shared this piece of wisdom with my friend Kelly Wahlquist as she was going through her own faith transformation. I've found it to be absolutely true in my own life too. I always wanted to be a communicator, and when I got into journalism it was a dream come true. But I needed to be a different kind of communicator in order to be truly happy and to fulfill God's will. So he eventually brought me, after much kicking and screaming, into Catholic media and communications.

I interviewed Kelly while writing this book, and I share her story because I think you might find it is a lot like your story and the stories of many others sitting next to you in the pew on Sunday. She says:

For me, it was mostly the busyness of life that got in the way of making a real connection to Jesus. But once I did, everything changed. I realized something was really missing in my life. I fell in love with Jesus and the Church and wanted to share that love of God with others, especially other busy women.

She is now one of the most sought-after Catholic speakers in the country, founder of the women's ministry WINE (Women in the New Evangelization).

Kelly's Story (in Kelly's Words)

I grew up your average Catholic — eight years of Catholic grade school, four years in a Catholic high school. We went to Mass as a family on Sundays and holy days, spent hours volunteering in the bingo tent at the fall fest, and brought casseroles and desserts to the lunch ladies when someone died. In fact, to this day our family still calls our pineapple-marshmallow concoction "funeral salad." I spent four years at a Catholic college and after graduation went on to yet another Catholic college for two years to get my degree in nursing. So, I had plenty of Catholic schooling, eighteen years to be exact, but somehow I didn't know much about my Catholic faith. Though I was, by society's standards, immersed in the Faith, my faith didn't trickle over into my life until I was thirty-three years old and bogged down juggling the daily demands of caring for a husband, three little kids, a dog … oh, and a job as a nursing supervisor.

My faith life radically changed one September day when a friend of mine made a bold move. I had been at Back to School Night at the Catholic grade school my preschooler and first-grader attended. (Yep, if I learned anything in my eighteen years of Catholic school, it was that my kids were going to follow the same path, though I really didn't know why.) After signing up to volunteer for somewhere under a million different committees, I was walking out of the school when a display of *The Great Adventure Bible Timeline* caught my eye. I stopped briefly to look at it, and instantly my friend Nichole came out from behind the table enthusiastically saying: "You have to do this! You have to do this Bible study by my friend Jeff Cavins. It's amazing!" My immediate reaction was: "Are you kidding me? If I sign up for one more thing, my husband will kill me." But Nichole persisted, "If you sign up, everyone will sign up." Noting she had no takers, I sadly said: "I'm sorry. I really can't."

The next morning, my friend Jozy called, saying, "Kelly, we saw you signed up for the Bible study, so forty of us signed up." I instantly called Nichole, who gave me all the good reasons why I should be in a Bible study, but it was her last three words that sealed the deal. She said, "And we have free child-care." Praise God! I'm in! Didn't really matter what book we were studying, but I guess the Bible was a plus.

My friend Jeff Cavins often says, "God gives us what we need wrapped in what we want." He's right. I wanted to have adult conversations. I wanted to have a place where I felt supported and encouraged by other women who were juggling families, and jobs, and life like I was. What I needed was a relationship with Jesus. Turns out, Nichole's bold move of signing me up for a Bible study, much to my chagrin (something to this day she says she can't believe she did), opened the door to a new relationship with Jesus and a newfound love for his Church ... and set the stage (or perhaps tilled the soil) for the sprouting of WINE.

Simply put, people are too busy. The demands of society today keep people so busy that faith is often dwindled down to something you check off your to-do list. Drive kids to soccer game, check. Pick up dry cleaning, check. Sign permission slip for field trip, check. Send "Save the Date" invite for gala, check. Go to Mass on Sunday, check.

There are also wounds that have caused people to turn away ... pain that has created a divide between them and their Creator — a distance that they may not even understand — and no matter how much they try to self-medicate or search for happiness in the things of this world, that pain continues and that wound grows deeper.

This is ultimately what the devil wants to do — to take our focus off God. To take our focus off the Creator and put it on the created. To spread our time thin, shatter our thoughts, and scatter our minds. This keeps us from living our faith and gives us reasons to rationalize our behavior. Deceiving someone into believing a lie about the Catholic faith is a much easier tactic than arguing with them when they have the Truth, because once you know the truth and beauty behind this magnificent Church Jesus created, there is no way you will want to be separated from it. In fact, it is the "field hospital," as Pope Francis said, that cleans up, heals, and restores any wound and warms the heart of the faithful!

I cannot think of anything more important than putting God first in all we do. I'm not saying it is easy, but there is nothing more important, because if we don't, we will find we are desperately grasping at a happiness we can never quite reach. We will experience a restlessness we can't quite comprehend.

From the moment we are created in the heart of the Father, we are all on a journey back to the heart of the Father. Saint Augustine said, "My heart is restless until it rests in Thee, O Lord." It is a journey based on relationship, experienced within relationship, and leading us back to the ultimate relationship, the relationship of the Most Holy Trinity. It is a journey from blessing to blessing.

While it may be true that our faith is about relationship, we have to remember that it is about a familial relationship of love. Our journey on earth is about finding our way back into the most perfect of all relationships, the Most Holy Trinity. God the Father loves us so much that he didn't leave us alone to find our way back to him. God gave his only-begotten Son to live among us, suffer with us, and die for us. God the Son loves us so much that he did the will of his Father ... and he didn't leave us alone to find our way back to him. Jesus established his Church on earth. In fact, Jesus told us that he was building his Church: "And I tell you, you are Peter, and on this rock I will build my Church, and the gates of Hades shall not prevail against it" (Mt 16:18).

Jesus established his Church on earth, and he put Peter in charge. And in Matthew 28:18–20, Jesus gives his apostles authority to rule and to teach, as well as apostolic succession. He gave us a loving earthly father to protect and guide us, and he gave us his mother in heaven to watch over us.

Your Story

Both Kelly and I broke through the busyness of our lives to the beautiful reality of living our faith beyond Sunday. Our stories are probably not that much different from yours. The places and the specific circumstances might be, but the bottom line is there are probably a lot of similarities. Kelly and I both had full lives, but not quite full enough.

We knew something, or more specifically someone, Jesus, was missing in our everyday experience. We were searching, as I suspect you might be as well.

That means your story is really just beginning. Don't let these final pages be the end. With the help of all the examples, suggestions, and resources on how to move forward, this could be and should be the beginning of an exciting faith adventure and a lifelong relationship with God. After all, it's God who gives us what we need wrapped in what we want, because that's the kind of God we serve. Everything we need and everything we could ever want is wrapped up in a relationship with Christ in the Catholic Church. He loves us that much. He can and will do the same for you, if you ask with a sincere and open heart. On top of everything God will give you, you will be able to give back to the world or pay it forward because you have the courage to go beyond Sunday.

As actor Jim Caviezel explained to those college students in Chicago, God loves you, and he knows the world needs you. You do and can continue to make a difference with your "yes":

> Callings come when we least expect them. I remember mine vividly. I had this experience. I was nineteen years old sitting in a movie theater.... The movie had ended, and out there in the darkness ... I had a sensation in my heart that made me think that I'm supposed to be an actor, that this is what God crafted me for, that this is what he wanted of me. Yes, my rational sense intervened. I knew nothing about acting; no agents, no managers, I can't memorize to save my life.... Yet I had a conviction. I had a call.

What would Jim Caviezel have missed had he given in to that "rational sense" and ignored that "sensation" in his heart? Where would the world be? *The Passion of the Christ* is still impacting millions of people more than fourteen years after its initial release.

And what about Saint Teresa of Calcutta? Most certainly, Mother Teresa, even had she ignored that "call within a call," would have served God for the rest of her life by staying with the Sisters of Loreto. But think about what the world at large would have missed. The Missionaries of Charity, which she founded in 1950, now has thousands of sisters serving the needy all over the globe. The religious order also runs schools, soup kitchens, and homeless shelters. Her sisters work with the poor, the elderly, people with AIDS, lepers, and oh, if that's not enough, Mother Teresa was a sought-after speaker far beyond religious circles. Her "call within a call" led to her meeting with world leaders and eventually being awarded the Nobel Peace Prize.

Go back to my invitation at the beginning of this book: *Come on in, the water's fine.* Jesus wants us to join him in walking on the water. He has big plans for each and every one us.

Or, as Pope Francis expressed it during his address on the feast of the Epiphany 2018: "We need to get up and go, not sit around but take risks, not stand still but set out." Like the three wise men, if we're really serious about making our faith part of our everyday lives, we need to leave our comfort zones and seek Jesus. "Jesus makes demands: he tells those who seek him to leave behind the armchair of worldly comforts and the reassuring warmth of hearth and home." But we can set out without fear, because we know that the Lord is with us, and that he "ensures peace and grants … 'exceedingly great joy' (Mt 2:10)."[29]

So what are we waiting for? Let's go! This journey of faith means that we have to have the courage of the Magi to set out on a journey. We need to ask for the courage of Saint Peter, or that of a nineteen-year-old kid sitting in a movie theater, to at least get out of the boat. Okay, so Saint Peter started to sink. And Jim Caviezel didn't become a movie star overnight. But you know the rest of Jim's story. And you probably know the rest of the story about Saint Peter, the rough-and-tumble Jewish fisherman who became the first pope. Jesus was right there to save him. He'll do the same for you, and then some — and not just on Sunday.

Anchors away! Surf's up! *Buon Viaggio!*

MONDAY

Reflect: Compare Kelly's journey to your own. What do you think Jesus might have in store for you? Are you willing to receive it?

TUESDAY

Pray: Today, pray the words of Saint Augustine of Hippo: "My heart is restless until it rests in Thee, O Lord."

WEDNESDAY

Journal: What makes you happy? What are your desires? Of the things you desire, what do you desire most from God? Why? Take some time to think and pray about this, and write your answers down.

THURSDAY

Pray: Place your desires in God's heart. Ask him to fulfill them for you and to show you how he is already giving you what you need wrapped up in the things you want.

FRIDAY

Reflect: Jesus is the ultimate gift of God to us — he gives us himself. Jesus is the gift that keeps on giving.

SATURDAY

Read: Reflect on where your faith box is today. Is it making a more regular appearance in your life? How does this make you feel? Where do you go from here?

Appendix

So Now What?

"Beyond Sunday" Resources

Maybe now you're raring to go but don't know exactly how to move forward. No worries. Take a deep breath and take your time going through the resources.

This appendix includes an extensive list that covers everything from Catholic Bible studies to basic catechetical programs. Whether you want to learn more in the privacy of your home or in a group setting, you have plenty of choices. I've created a list of some of the resources I think are best suited to help people take their faith beyond Sunday morning and into their daily lives. Feel free to pick and choose what you think is best for you — and you can always come back for more ideas down the road.

My suggestion before you go over this list is to take some time to pray about where you feel God is calling you. If you feel you need to learn more in general about what the Church teaches, I would consider ChristLife. If you have a love of Scripture and want to get a better understanding of how it applies to your daily life, pick up one of the daily devotionals recommended here, such as *The Word Among Us* or *Magnificat*.

I also highly recommend that you stay connected to the Catholic world through faithful media outlets such as Ave Maria Radio, Relevant Radio, and EWTN, along with great websites, podcasts, and other media that can keep you up-to-date on all things Catholic.

Open your heart. Ask for God's guidance. Take one step at a time and don't forget to enjoy the faith journey.

"Beyond Sunday" Resource List

Catholic News Outlets

- *Our Sunday Visitor:* www.osv.com
- *National Catholic Register:* www.ncregister.com
- *Catholic News Service:* www.catholicnews.com
- *EWTN News:* www.ewtnnews.com
- *EWTN News Nightly:* http://www.ewtn.com/tv/live /ewtnnewsnightly.asp
- *Catholic News Agency:* www.catholicnewsagency.com
- *Zenit News Agency:* www.zenit.org
- *Aleteia:* www.aleteia.org
- *The Good News:* www.thegoodnewsletter.org

Catholic Broadcast Media

- *Ave Maria Radio:* www.avemariaradio.net
- *Eternal Word Television Network (EWTN):* www.ewtn.com
- *Relevant Radio:* www.relevantradio.com
- *Vatican Radio:* http://en.radiovaticana.va/

Catholic Magazines/Periodicals

- *OSV Newsweekly:* https://www.osv.com/OSVNewsweekly.aspx
- *L'Osservatore Romano:* https://subscribe.osv.com/LOR/?f=paid
- *Take Out: Family Faith on the Go:* https://subscribe.osv.com /TOT/?f=paid
- *National Catholic Register:* http://www.ncregister.com/
- *Crisis Magazine:* www.CrisisMagazine.com
- *Catholic World Report:* www.CatholicWorldReport.com
- *First Things:* www.firstthings.com
- *Marian Helper Magazine:* http://www.marian.org /marianhelper/

Popular Catholic Websites/Blogs

- *EWTN:* www.EWTN.com
- *Catholic Answers:* https://www.catholic.com/
- *Integrated Catholic Life:* www.integratedcatholiclife.org
- *Patheos:* www.patheos.com/catholic
- *New Advent:* www.NewAdvent.org
- *Catholic News & Inspiration (Patti Maguire Armstrong):* http:// www.pattimaguirearmstrong.com/

Daily Devotionals

- *Magnificat:* www.magnificat.net
- *The Word Among Us:* www.wau.org
- *One Bread, One Body:* www.presentationministries.com

Examination of Conscience

- *Daily Examination of Conscience:* https://www.ewtn.com/library/prayer/examconscience.htm
- *Ignatian Spirituality's Daily Examen:* https://www.ignatianspirituality.com/ignatian-prayer/the-examen
- *Examination of Conscience by Fr. John Hardon, S.J.:* https://www.ewtn.com/library/SPIRIT/EXAMCONS.TXT

Bible/Group Studies

- *Catholic Scripture Study International:* www.cssprogram.net
- *Great Adventure Catholic Bible Study:* www.biblestudyforcatholics.com
- *Dr. Scott Hahn's online Bible studies:* https://stpaulcenter.com/studies-tools/online-studies/
- *Father Mitch Pacwa, S.J.'s "A Bible Study Guide for Catholics" series:* www.osvcatholicbookstore.com/OSVAuthors/FatherMitchPacwaSJ.aspx

Resources for Catholic Men

- *Valiant magazine:* https://www.osvcatholicbookstore.com/Newsstand/Valiant.aspx
- *Be a Man! Father Larry Richards:* http://thereasonforourhope.org/shop/beaman2/
- *Knights of Columbus:* http://www.kofc.org/en/
- *National Fellowship of Catholic Men:* https://www.facebook.com/National-Fellowship-of-Catholic-Men-NFCM-341215802556086/
- *St. Joseph Covenant Keepers (Steve Wood):* http://dads.org/
- *Those Catholic Men:* www.thosecatholicmen.com
- *The Catholic Gentleman:* https://www.catholicgentleman.net/
- *That Man Is You (TMIY):* https://www.catholicmensministry.com/tmiy
- *Real Men Pray The Rosary (David Cavillo):* www.realmenpraytherosary.org
- *Rise (30-Day Challenge for Catholic Men):* www.MenRiseUp.org

- *Integrity Starts Here (helping men break free from porn addiction):* http://peterkleponis.com/AboutIntegrityStartsHere
- *Courage (for those struggling with same-sex attraction):* https://couragerc.org/

Resources for Catholic Women

- *Radiant magazine:* https://www.osvcatholicbookstore.com/Newsstand/Radiant.aspx
- *Women of Grace (Johnnette Benkovic):* www.WomenofGrace.com
- *EWTN's The Catholic View for Women:* www.TheCatholicViewForWomen.com
- *WINE — Women in the New Evangelization:* www.CatholicVineyard.com
- *CatholicMom.com (Lisa Hendey):* www.CatholicMom.com
- *Catholic Mom's Café (Donna-Marie Cooper O'Boyle):* http://catholicmomscafe.blogspot.com/
- *Blessed Is She:* www.blessedisshe.net
- *Women of Grace Foundational Study:* www.WomenofGrace.com
- *Walking with Purpose Bible study:* www.walkingwithpurpose.com
- *Women Speak for Themselves:* https://womenspeakforthemselves.com/
- *Catholic Women's Forum:* https://catholicwomensforum.org/
- *From Pope Saint John Paul II:*
  - *Letter to Women:* https://w2.vatican.va/content/john-paul-ii/en/letters/1995/documents/hf_jp-ii_let_29061995_women.html
  - *Mulieris Dignitatem (The Dignity and Vocation of Women):* https://w2.vatican.va/content/john-paul-ii/en/apost_letters/1988/documents/hf_jp-ii_apl_19880815_mulieris-dignitatem.html
  - *Redemptoris Mater ("Mother of the Redeemer"):* http://w2.vatican.va/content/john-paul-ii/en/encyclicals/documents/hf_jp-ii_enc_25031987_redemptoris-mater.html
- *ENDOW (Educating on the Nature and Dignity of Women):* http://www.endowgroups.org/
- *Courage (for those struggling with same-sex attraction):* https://couragerc.org/

Resources on Marriage
- *The Alexander House (Julie and Greg Alexander):* www .TheAlexanderHouse.org
- *Institute for Marital Healing (Dr. Richard Fitzgibbons):* www .MaritalHealing.com
- *Marriage Encounter:* www.WWME.org
- *Retrouvaille (for troubled Catholic Marriages):* https:// retrouvaille.org/
- *Beloved (Augustine Institute):* https://www.augustineinstitute .org/formed/beloved/
- *Intimate Graces (Teresa Tomeo and Deacon Dominick Pastore):* www.TeresaTomeo.com
- *Rose Sweet:* www.RoseSweet.com
- *Restoring Trust (for couples struggling with porn in their Marriage):* www.peterkleponis.com/restoringtrust

Resources for Teens/Young Adults
- *EWTN's Life on the Rock:* http://www.ewtn.com/tv/live /lifeontherock.asp
- *FOCUS — Fellowship of Catholic University Students:* www .Focus.org
- *Young Catholic Professionals:* http://www .youngcatholicprofessionals.org/
- *Theology on Tap:* http://www.renewtot.org/
- *Life Teen:* www.lifeteen.com
- *Net Ministries:* http://www.netusa.org/
- *Steubenville Youth and Young Adult Conferences:* https:// steubenvilleconferences.com/
- *The Culture Project:* www.restoreculture.com
- *Creatio:* www.creatio.org

Evangelization Programs/Ministries
- *ChristLife Catholic Ministry for Evangelization:* www.christlife.org
- *FORMED (Augustine Institute):* https://www .augustineinstitute.org/formed/
- *Real Life Catholic (Chris Stefanick):* www.RealLifeCatholic.com
- *Unleash the Gospel (Archbishop Allen H. Vigneron, Archdiocese of Detroit):* http://www.unleashthegospel.org/
- *The Coming Home Network (Marcus Grodi):* https://chnetwork.org
- *New Leaven:* http://www.newleaven.org/

- *Ignatius Productions (a teaching apostolate of Father Mitch Pacwa, S.J.):* www.FatherMitchPacwa.org
- *Crossroads Initiative (Dr. Marcellino D'Ambrosio):* www .crossroadsinitiative.com/

Catholic Retreats/Centers
- *Cursillo:* https://www.natl-cursillo.org/
- *Malvern Retreat House:* https://www.malvernretreat.com/
- *Life in the Spirit Seminar/Catholic Charismatic Renewal:* http:// www.nsc-chariscenter.org/
- *Christ Renews His Parish:* http://www.mychrp.com/MYCRHP /Welcome.html

Continuing Catholic Education
- *Avila Institute:* https://avila-institute.com/
- *Augustine Institute:* https://www.augustineinstitute.org/
- *Lighthouse Catholic Media (Augustine Institute):* https://www .lighthousecatholicmedia.org/
- *Catholic Courses (Saint Benedict Press/Tan Books):* https:// www.tanbooks.com/catholic-courses.html
- *Symbolon (Augustine Institute):* https://www .lighthousecatholicmedia.org/symbolon
- *Catholicism (Bishop Robert Barron):* http://catholicism .wordonfire.org/
- *St. Paul Center for Continuing Education (Dr. Scott Hahn):* https://stpaulcenter.com/

Pro-Life Resources
- *March for Life:* http://marchforlife.org/
- *Priests for Life:* http://www.priestsforlife.org/
- *LifeNews:* http://www.lifenews.com/
- *LifeSiteNews:* https://www.lifesitenews.com/
- *Silent No More Awareness Campaign:* http:// silentnomoreawareness.org/
- *Rachel's Vineyard:* http://www.rachelsvineyard.org/

Catholic Pilgrimages
- *Corporate Travel Services:* www.CTSCentral.net
- *T's Italy:* Traveling to Italy with Teresa Tomeo in Your Pocket: www.TeresaTomeo.com/Italy

- *Footprints of God (Steve Ray):* www
  .FootprintsofGodPilgrimages.com

Catholic Podcasts
- *Discerning Hearts:* https://player.fm/series/discerning-hearts
  -catholic-podcasts
- *Word on Fire (Bishop Robert Barron):* http://wordonfireshow
  .com/
- *Catholic Answers Live:* https://www.catholic.com/audio
  /podcasts
- *Jennifer Fulwiler:* www.jenniferfulwiler.com/
- *iPadre (Father Jay Finelli):* https://player.fm/series/ipadre
  -catholic-podcast
- *The Reason for Our Hope (Father Larry Richards):* https://
  player.fm/series/the-reason-for-our-hope-weekly-homilies
- *Father John Riccardo Podcasts:* https://player.fm/series/fr-john
  -riccardos-podcasts

Catholic Apps
- *Laudate*
- *MassTimes*
- *EWTN*
- *Ave Maria Radio*
- *Magnificat*
- *Relevant Radio*
- *Holy Rosary*
- *Divine Mercy*
- *Chaplets (Android); Chaplets and Rosary (Apple)*

Important Daily Prayers

Apostles' Creed
I believe in God,
the Father Almighty,
Creator of heaven and earth,
and in Jesus Christ, His only Son, our Lord,
who was conceived by the Holy Spirit,
born of the Virgin Mary,
suffered under Pontius Pilate,

was crucified, died and was buried;
he descended into hell;
on the third day he rose again from the dead;
he ascended into heaven,
is seated at the right hand
    of God the Father almighty;
from there he will come to judge
    the living and the dead.
I believe in the Holy Spirit,
the holy catholic Church,
the communion of saints,
the forgiveness of sins,
the resurrection of the body,
and life everlasting. Amen.[30]

The Lord's Prayer (Our Father)

Our Father, who art in heaven,
hallowed by thy name;
thy kingdom come;
thy will be done
on earth as it is in heaven.
Give us this day our daily bread;
and forgive us our trespasses
as we forgive those
who trespass against us;
and lead us not into temptation,
but deliver us from evil.
Amen.

Hail Mary

Hail Mary, full of grace.
The Lord is with thee.
Blessed art thou among women,
and blessed is the fruit of thy womb, Jesus.

Holy Mary, Mother of God,
pray for us sinners,
now and at the hour of our death.
Amen.

The Glory Be

Glory be to the Father,
and to the Son,
and to the Holy Spirit.

As it was in the beginning,
is now, and ever shall be,
world without end.
Amen.

Guardian Angel Prayer

Angel of God, my guardian dear, to whom God's love commits me here,
ever this day be at my side, to light and guard, to rule and guide. Amen.

St. Michael the Archangel

St. Michael the Archangel, defend us in battle; be our defense against
the wickedness and snares of the devil. May God rebuke him, we
humbly pray; and do thou, O Prince of the heavenly host, by the power
of God, thrust into hell Satan and the other evil spirits who prowl about
the world seeking the ruin of souls. Amen.

Memorare

Remember, O most gracious Virgin Mary, that never was it known that
anyone who fled to your protection, implored your help, or sought your
intercession was left unaided.

Inspired by this confidence I fly unto you, O virgin of virgins, my
Mother. To you do I come, before you I stand, sinful and sorrowful. O
Mother of the Word Incarnate, despise not my petitions, but in your
mercy, hear and answer me. Amen.

Hail, Holy Queen

Hail, holy Queen, Mother of Mercy. Hail, our life, our sweetness and
our hope. To you do we cry, poor banished children of Eve. To you do
we send up our sighs, mourning, and weeping in this valley of tears.
Turn, then, most gracious advocate, your eyes of mercy toward us, and
after this, our exile, show unto us the blessed fruit of your womb, Jesus.
O clement, O loving, O sweet Virgin Mary.

Morning Offering

O Jesus, through the Immaculate Heart of Mary, I offer you my prayers, works, joys, and sufferings of this day for all the intentions of your Sacred Heart, in union with the Holy Sacrifice of the Mass throughout the world, for the salvation of souls, the reparation of sins, the reunion of all Christians, and in particular for the intentions of the Holy Father this month. Amen.

Act of Contrition

My God, I am sorry for my sins with all my heart. In choosing to do wrong and failing to do good, I have sinned against you whom I should love above all things.

I firmly intend, with your help, to do penance, to sin no more, and to avoid whatever leads me to sin. Our Savior Jesus Christ suffered and died for us. In his name, my God, have mercy.

The Angelus

V. The angel of the Lord declared unto Mary;
R. And she conceived by the Holy Spirit.
   Hail, Mary ...

V. Behold the handmaid of the Lord.
R. Be it done unto me according to your word.
   Hail, Mary ...

V. And the Word was made flesh,
R. And dwelt among us.
   Hail, Mary ...

V. Pray for us, O holy Mother of God,
R. That we may be made worthy of the promises of Christ.

Let us pray: Pour forth, we beseech you, O Lord, your grace into our hearts, that we, to whom the incarnation of Christ, your Son, was made known by the message of an angel, may by his passion and cross be brought to the glory of his resurrection, through the same Christ our Lord.

R. Amen.

The Holy Rosary
Even offering one decade of the Rosary each day is a powerful way to grow in your faith. Learn how to pray the Rosary here: https://www.ewtn.com/devotionals/prayers/rosary/.

Prayer Before Communion
Lord Jesus Christ, Son of the living God, have mercy on me, a sinner.

Prayer Before Meals
Bless us, O Lord, and these thy gifts which we are about to receive from thy bounty. Through Christ Our Lord. Amen.

Prayer After Meals
We give Thee thanks for all Thy benefits, O Almighty God, who livest and reignest world without end. Amen. May the souls of the faithful departed, through the mercy of God, rest in peace. Amen.

Evening Examination of Conscience
What sins have I committed today in thought, word, deed, and omission against God, my neighbor, and myself?

Prayer of Saint Francis
Lord, make me an instrument of your peace:
Where there is hatred, let me sow love.
Where there is injury, pardon,
Where there is doubt, faith,
Where there is despair, hope,
Where there is darkness, light,
and where there is sadness, joy.

O Divine Master, grant that I may not so much seek
    to be consoled, as to console;
To be understood, as to understand;
To be loved, as to love;
For it is in giving that we receive,
It is in pardoning that we are pardoned
And it is in dying that we are born to eternal life.

Fátima Prayer

O my Jesus, forgive us our sins, save us from the fires of hell. Lead all souls to heaven, especially those most in need of thy mercy.

Divine Mercy

Jesus, I trust in you!

(You can learn more about the Divine Mercy Message and Chaplet at http://www.usccb.org/beliefs-and-teachings/how-weteach/new-evangelization/year-of-faith/how-to-pray-the-chaplet-of-divinemercy.cfm)

Pardon Prayer
(taught by the Angel to the three children at Fátima)
"My God, I believe, I adore, I hope, and I love you! I beg pardon for those who do not believe, do not adore, do not hope, and do not love you." *(Repeat three times.)*

* *

Ways to Help Us Live Out and Grow in Our Catholic Faith

Corporal Works of Mercy
- Feed the hungry
- Give drink to the thirsty
- Clothe the naked
- Shelter the homeless
- Visit the sick
- Visit the imprisoned
- Bury the dead

Spiritual Works of Mercy
- Counsel the doubtful
- Instruct the ignorant
- Admonish the sinner
- Comfort the afflicted
- Forgive all offenses
- Bear wrongs patiently
- Pray for the living and the dead

Cardinal Virtues (Taken from CCC 1806–1809)
PRUDENCE
1806 *Prudence* is the virtue that disposes practical reason to discern our true good in every circumstance and to choose the right means of achieving it; "the prudent man looks where he is going" (Prov 14:15). "Keep sane and sober for your prayers" (1 Pet 4:7). Prudence is "right reason in action," writes St. Thomas Aquinas, following Aristotle (St. Thomas Aquinas, *STh* II–II, 47, 2). It is not to be confused with timidity or fear, nor with duplicity or dissimulation. It is called *auriga virtutum* (the charioteer of the virtues); it guides the other virtues by setting rule and measure. It is prudence that immediately guides the judgment of conscience. The prudent man determines and directs his conduct in accordance with this judgment. With the help of this virtue we apply moral principles to particular cases without error and overcome doubts about the good to achieve and the evil to avoid.

JUSTICE
1807 *Justice* is the moral virtue that consists in the constant and firm will to give their due to God and neighbor. Justice toward God is called the "virtue of religion." Justice toward men disposes one to respect the rights of each and to establish in human relationships the harmony that promotes equity with regard to persons and to the common good. The just man, often mentioned in the Sacred Scriptures, is distinguished by habitual right thinking and the uprightness of his conduct toward his neighbor.

FORTITUDE
1808 *Fortitude* is the moral virtue that ensures firmness in difficulties and constancy in the pursuit of the good. It strengthens the resolve to resist temptations and to overcome obstacles in the moral life. The virtue of fortitude enables one to conquer fear, even fear of death, and to face trials and persecutions. It disposes one even to renounce and sacrifice his life in defense of a just cause.

TEMPERANCE
1809 *Temperance* is the moral virtue that moderates the attraction of pleasures and provides balance in the use of created goods. It ensures the will's mastery over instincts and keeps desires within the limits of what is honorable. The temperate person directs the sensitive appetites toward what is good and maintains a healthy discretion: "Do not follow your inclination and strength, walking according to the desires of your heart" (Sir 5:2; cf 37:27–31).

Theological Virtues (Taken from CCC 1814, 1817, and 1822)

FAITH

1814 *Faith* is the theological virtue by which we believe in God and believe all that he has said and revealed to us, and that Holy Church proposes for our belief, because he is truth itself. By faith "man freely commits his entire self to God" (*DV* 5). For this reason the believer seeks to know and do God's will.

HOPE

1817 *Hope* is the theological virtue by which we desire the kingdom of heaven and eternal life as our happiness, placing our trust in Christ's promises and relying not on our own strength, but on the help of the grace of the Holy Spirit.

CHARITY

1822 *Charity* is the theological virtue by which we love God above all things for his own sake, and our neighbor as ourselves for the love of God.

Gifts of The Holy Spirit

The seven gifts of the Holy Spirit, which we receive at baptism and which are strengthened within us at confirmation, are:

- Wisdom
- Understanding
- Counsel
- Fortitude
- Knowledge
- Piety
- Fear of the Lord

Fruits of the Holy Spirit

The tradition of the Church lists twelve fruits of the Holy Spirit:

- Charity
- Joy
- Peace
- Patience
- Kindness
- Goodness
- Generosity
- Gentleness
- Faithfulness
- Modesty
- Self-control
- Chastity

The Beatitudes

1716 The Beatitudes are at the heart of Jesus' preaching. They take up the promises made to the chosen people since Abraham. The Beatitudes fulfill the promises by ordering them no longer merely to the possession of a territory, but to the Kingdom of heaven:

> Blessed are the poor in spirit, for theirs is the kingdom of heaven.
> Blessed are those who mourn, for they shall be comforted.
> Blessed are the meek, for they shall inherit the earth.
> Blessed are those who hunger and thirst for righteousness, for they shall be satisfied.
> Blessed are the merciful, for they shall obtain mercy.
> Blessed are the pure in heart, for they shall see God.
> Blessed are the peacemakers, for they shall be called sons of God.
> Blessed are those who are persecuted for righteousness' sake, for theirs is the kingdom of heaven.
> Blessed are you when men revile you and persecute you and utter all kinds of evil against you falsely on my account.
> Rejoice and be glad,
> for your reward is great in heaven. (Mt 5:3–12)

Stay Connected with "Beyond Sunday" Happenings!

Visit the Beyond Sunday website and sign up for our Beyond Sunday news and other resources that will help you live out and grow in your faith: **www.OSV.com/BeyondSunday**.

Schedule a "Beyond Sunday" Mission at Your Parish!

Invite Teresa Tomeo and Gail Coniglio to your parish for a Beyond Sunday mission. Send speaking inquiries to: **BeyondSunday@osv.com**.

Notes

1. Pope John Paul II, Message of the Holy Father John Paul II to the Youth of the World on the Occasion of the XIX World Youth Day 2004 (February 22, 2004): http://w2.vatican.va/content/john-paul-ii /en/messages/youth/documents/hf_jp-ii_mes_20040301_xix-world -youth-day.html.

2. Archbishop Allen Vigneron, 2016 pastoral letter, *Unleash the Gospel*, p. 9: http://www.unleashthegospel.org/.

3. Pope Paul VI, *Evangelii Nuntiandi* (Evangelization in the Modern World) (December 8, 1975), 14: http://w2.vatican.va/content/paul -vi/en/apost_exhortations/documents/hf_p-vi_exh_19751208 _evangelii-nuntiandi.html.

4. From *The Roman Missal*, 144.

5. Pope Francis, General Audience (December 13, 2017): https://press.vatican.va/content/salastampa/en/bollettino /pubblico/2017/12/13/171213a.html.

6. Pope Francis, General Audience (December 20, 2017): https:// w2.vatican.va/content/francesco/en/audiences/2017/documents/papa -francesco_20171220_udienza-generale.html.

7. Ibid.

8. Pope Francis, Homily (May 10, 2013): http://www.lastampa .it/2013/05/10/esteri/vatican-insider/en/pope-francis-christian-joy-is -a-gift-from-jesus-FEWTN0rCL8J8R3q93jv6qL/pagina.html.

9. Archbishop Allen Vigneron, *Unleash the Gospel*, p. 15.

10. Pope Benedict XVI, Message of His Holiness Pope Benedict XVI on the Occasion of the Sixth Ordinary Assembly of the International Forum of Catholic Action (August 10, 2012): https://w2.vatican.va /content/benedict-xvi/en/messages/pont-messages/2012/documents /hf_ben-xvi_mes_20120810_fiac.html.

11. Pope Francis, Letter of His Holiness Pope Francis According to Which an Indulgence Is Granted to the Faithful on the Occasion of the Extraordinary Jubilee of Mercy (September 1, 2015): https://w2.vatican.va/content/francesco/en/letters/2015/documents/papa-francesco_20150901_lettera-indulgenza-giubileo-misericordia.html.

12. Pope Francis, General Audience (March 30, 2016): https://w2.vatican.va/content/francesco/en/audiences/2016/documents/papa-francesco_20160330_udienza-generale.html.

13. Pope Francis, Angelus address (June 30, 2013): http://en.radiovaticana.va/storico/2013/06/30/pope_francis_sunday_angelus_(full_text)/en1-706181.

14. Pew Research Center, "Religion in Everyday Life" (April 12, 2016): http://www.pewforum.org/2016/04/12/religion-in-everyday-life/.

15. "Conscience," *Catholic Dictionary*, https://www.catholicculture.org/culture/library/dictionary/index.cfm?id=32755.

16. Pope Francis, Angelus address (June 30, 2013).

17. Oliver Darcy, "New York Times executive editor: 'We don't get religion,'" *Business Insider* (December 9, 2016): http://www.businessinsider.com/new-york-times-editor-religion-dean-baquet-2016-12.

18. Greg Erlandson, "Engaging Catholic media for hearing the Church's voice," *Legatus Magazine* (January 2018): http://legatus.org/engaging-catholic-media-for-hearing-the-churchs-voice/.

19. Archbishop John P. Foley, Pastoral Instruction *"Aetatis Novae"* on Social Communications on the Twentieth Anniversary of *Communio et Progressio* (February 22, 1992), 4: http://www.vatican.va/roman_curia/pontifical_councils/pccs/documents/rc_pc_pccs_doc_22021992_aetatis_en.html.

20. Pope Francis, Angelus address (June 30, 2013).

21. Cardinal Joseph Ratzinger, Homily of His Eminence Card. Joseph Ratzinger, Dean of the College of Cardinals (April 18, 2005): http://www.vatican.va/gpII/documents/homily-pro-eligendo-pontifice_20050418_en.html.

22. Archbishop Allen Vigneron, *Unleash the Gospel*, p. 24.

23. Pope John Paul II, *Ecclesia de Eucharistia* ("The Church from the Eucharist") (April 17 2003), 1 (emphasis in original): http://www.vatican.va/holy_father/special_features/encyclicals/documents/hf_jp-ii_enc_20030417_ecclesia_eucharistia_en.html.

24. Archbishop Samuel J. Aquila, "Ending harassment requires more than laws," *Denver Catholic* (December 5, 2017): http://denvercatholic.org /ending-harassment-requires-laws/.

25. Pope John Paul II, "The Media and the Family: A Risk and a Richness" (May 23, 2004): http://w2.vatican.va/content/john-paul-ii /en/messages/communications/documents/hf_jp-ii_mes_20040124 _world-communications-day.html.

26. Archbishop Allen Vigneron, *Unleash the Gospel*, p. 21.

27. Pope Benedict XVI, Homily (September 10, 2006): http://w2.vatican .va/content/benedict-xvi/en/homilies/2006/documents/hf_ben-xvi _hom_20060910_neue-messe-munich.html.

28. "Why Do Social Networks Increase Stress?" *Huffington Post* (July 12, 2013; updated December 6, 2017): https://www.huffingtonpost.com /john-dick/social-networks-and-stress_b_3534170.html.

29. Pope Francis, Homily (January 6, 2018): https://press.vatican.va /content/salastampa/en/bollettino/pubblico/2018/01/06/180106a .html.

30. From *The Roman Missal*, 19.

Special Thanks

*Thank you to Greg Willits, Mary Beth Baker, Terry Poplava,
Jill Adamson, Tracy Stewart, and the entire
Our Sunday Visitor team for their amazing support and for embracing
the Beyond Sunday movement in order to help save souls.*

BEYOND SUNDAY
STUDY GUIDE

By Teresa Tomeo and Gail Coniglio

The **Beyond Sunday Study Guide** is the companion to Teresa Tomeo's **Beyond Sunday: Becoming a 24/7 Catholic**. This eight-week study guide is designed to help you live your faith beyond Sunday in your everyday life, with a community of people seeking growth in faith alongside you. Each week provides prayers, reflection questions, a "Holy Habits of the Week" challenge, the story of an inspirational person or saint, and lined pages for your notes. This is just the beginning of your journey to a richly rewarding life of faith. **(Inventory No. X1930)**

To Order from Our Sunday Visitor
Call: 800-348-2440
Fax: 800-498-6709
Online: OSVCatholicBookstore.com